1 MONTH OF FREE READING

at

www.ForgottenBooks.com

By purchasing this book you are eligible for one month membership to ForgottenBooks.com, giving you unlimited access to our entire collection of over 1,000,000 titles via our web site and mobile apps.

To claim your free month visit:

www.forgottenbooks.com/free19871

* Offer is valid for 45 days from date of purchase. Terms and conditions apply.

ISBN 978-0-483-52086-8
PIBN 10019871

This book is a reproduction of an important historical work. Forgotten Books uses
state-of-the-art technology to digitally reconstruct the work, preserving the original format
whilst repairing imperfections present in the aged copy. In rare cases, an imperfection in
the original, such as a blemish or missing page, may be replicated in our edition. We do,
however, repair the vast majority of imperfections successfully; any imperfections that
remain are intentionally left to preserve the state of such historical works.

Forgotten Books is a registered trademark of FB &c Ltd.
Copyright © 2018 FB &c Ltd.
FB &c Ltd, Dalton House, 60 Windsor Avenue, London, SW19 2RR.
Company number 08720141. Registered in England and Wales.

For support please visit www.forgottenbooks.com

THE MODERN HEBREW,

AND

THE HEBREW CHRISTIAN.

BY

REV. ELIESER BASSIN, C.M. & Ph.B.,

MISSIONARY IN JASSY, ROUMANIA;

EDITOR OF THE "EINTRACHT" (GERMAN); AUTHOR OF "A FINGER-POST TO THE WAY OF SALVATION" (ENGLISH); "THREEFOLD CORD" (HEBREW); "ELIESER'S VOICE" HEBREW); "THE JEWISH QUESTION" (GERMAN), ETC. ETC.

LONDON:
JAMES NISBET & CO., 21 BERNERS STREET.
1882.

[All Rights Reserved.]

EDINBURGH:
PRINTED BY LORIMER AND GILLIES,
31 ST. ANDREW SQUARE.

PREFATORY NOTES.

"I HAVE read Mr. Bassin's narrative with much interest and not a little benefit. The first part gives details on many points of Jewish life, of which we are very ignorant, but on which it is useful for us to have information. The state of Jewish belief and opinion on religious subjects is brought out very fully. The second part has a remarkable interest of its own,—the reader is carried on from chapter to chapter with a profound interest in Mr. Bassin's experience and treatment, and an eager desire to know how the story is to end. From all I have seen of Mr. Bassin, as a student in one of my classes in the New College, and otherwise, I have been led to form a high opinion of his scholarship, his abilities, and his Christian sincerity.

"W. G. BLAIKIE, D.D.

"NEW COLLEGE, EDINBURGH,
 "30th March, 1882."

"IN accordance with Professor Blaikie's testimony to Mr. Elieser Bassin's narrative, I have to express the great interest with which I have read it, and my conviction that it cannot fail to interest and inform a large circle of readers who care for all that concerns the race of Israel,—that old nation which is every year taking a place of increased importance in the human family, whose past has been by the Lord so deeply worked in the history of our redemption, and whose future is so closely bound up with the salvation of the world.

"A. MOODY STUART, D.D."

CONTENTS.

Part I.

THE MODERN HEBREW; OR, THE TALMUDIST AND CABALIST.

AN ACCOUNT OF THE TRADITIONS, CUSTOMS, MANNERS, AND CEREMONIES OF THE JEWS IN GENERAL, AND OF RUSSIAN AND POLISH JEWS IN PARTICULAR, TOGETHER WITH THE AUTHOR'S EARLY LIFE.

CHAPTER I.
PAGE
My Birthplace, my Parents, and my Childhood, ... 3

CHAPTER II.
My first Boarding-School, and a Glimpse at some Jewish Superstitions,

CHAPTER III.
My highly-esteemed Tutor; Thirteen Articles of the Jewish Faith, and a Specimen of the most important Daily Prayers, ... 12

CHAPTER IV.
The Talmud and its Origin, ... 19

CONTENTS.

CHAPTER V.
Leave-taking of my Tutor on his being called to be a Rabbi, and the Consecration of the New Moon, ... 24

CHAPTER VI.
The Duties of the Rabbi, and the Divorce Ceremony, ... 28

CHAPTER VII.
The Ceremony of Circumcision, and Redemption of the First-born, . . 33

CHAPTER VIII.
My establishing a Society for the Clothing of Poor Children; Confirmation at the Age of Thirteen; and my First Sermon in the Synagogue, . . 40

CHAPTER IX.
A Boy's Extraordinary Journey in order to visit Miracle-performing Rabbis, and the Demon in a Cellar, ... 44

CHAPTER X.
Rabbi Hillel; Description of a Jeshivah—*i.e.*, Rabbinical College; and the Jewish Calendar, ... 52

CHAPTER XI.
The Feast of the New Year; The Fast of Gedaliah; The Days of Penitence, and the Day of Atonement, ... 56

CHAPTER XII.
The Feast of Tabernacles; Hosanna Rabba, and Simchath Toura, . . . 65

CHAPTER XIII.
The Feast of Dedication; The Fast of the Tenth of Teveth; The Fast of Esther; and the Feast of Purim, ... 70

CONTENTS.

CHAPTER XIV.

The Month Nisan; The Feast of the Passover; The Feast of Pentecost; The Fast of the Seventeenth of Tamuz; and the Strict Fast of the Ninth of Ab, ... 75

CHAPTER XV.

Celebration of the Jewish Sabbath, ... 84

CHAPTER XVI.

My further Connection with Rabbi Hillel; Two Journeys to the Grand Rabbi of the Jewish Sect called Chabad, and a Description of the Sect, ... 92

CHAPTER XVII.

How I tried to establish a New Jewish Sect; My Studies in the Grand Rabbinical Academy of Valosin; The Jewish Theology in general, and the Chabad in particular, ... 100

CHAPTER XVIII.

Jewish Marriages—their Tradition and Celebration. ... 115

CHAPTER XIX.

My Dissatisfaction with the Religious State of the Jews; Travelling for a Year in Russia; Preaching with a View to Reformation amongst the Jews; My Acquaintance with the Sect called Karaites; Disputes with their chief Chacham, ... 120

CHAPTER XX.

My occupying the Office of a Rabbi during the Illness and after the Death of my Cousin; Religious Ceremonies connected with Illness, Death, Burial, and Mourning; A Strange Tale connected with the Prayer for the Dead, ... 127

CHAPTER XXI.

Disruption of the Sect Chabad; Reasons why I was considered by some Jews as a Miracle-Performer; My Journey to the East; Arrival in Constantinople; The Jews warn me of the Missionaries, ... 136

Part II.

THE HEBREW CHRISTIAN.

AN ACCOUNT OF HOW THE AUTHOR WAS PRIVILEGED, NOT ONLY TO BELIEVE IN CHRIST, BUT ALSO TO SUFFER FOR HIS SAKE, AND TO TESTIFY OF HIS GRACE TO JEWS AND GENTILES. ALSO, A GLIMPSE INTO THE CORRUPTION OF THE RUSSIAN GOVERNMENT OFFICIALS IN THE NINETEENTH CENTURY.

CHAPTER I.

My Acquaintance with the Missionaries ; A Conversation concerning the Messiah ; The Jewish History of Christ ; My Conversion and Baptism ; A Letter from the Rev. A. Tomory to the Jewish Mission Committee ; Intimation to my Relations of my finding the expected Messiah ; Letter from Rev. A. Tomory to F. Brown-Douglas, Esq., ... 145

CHAPTER II.

My Zeal in Preaching the Gospel ; A Severe Illness ; Engagement as Teacher in the Mission School ; Arrival of a Jewish Deputy from Russia to confer with me ; By Bribery of Jewish Gold I was made Prisoner and conveyed on board a Russian Vessel to Odessa ; Extract from the *Free Church Record* of December 1869, ... 151

CHAPTER III.

The Jewish Triumph ; My Answer to their Triumph ; The Terrible Night ; The Tempter ; Help and Strength from the Lord, ... 157

CHAPTER IV.

My First Visitors in the Prison bring me Good Tidings ; My Second Visitors come with Threatenings ; My Removal to the Common Prison ; I am taken to confer with the Rabbi ; I dispute with him in Presence of many Jews ; The Kindness of the Rabbi to me ; My Removal from Odessa to Balta, ... 163

CONTENTS.

CHAPTER V.

Four Days in the Prison at Balta; From Balta to Olwiopol; A Week's Imprisonment; From Olwiopol to Uman; Address to the Peasants; Peculiar Interview with an Innkeeper; Arrival in Uman; Notes from the *Free Church Record*, ... 169

CHAPTER VI.

Further Troubles; I am unable to proceed; A few Days' Rest in the Hospital at Winnagrodca; Our March renewed; Arrival at Kiev; An Interview with my Uncle; His Fruitless Efforts to make me turn from Christianity; Inward Conflicts and Final Victory; A Visit in Prison from my Uncle and other Jews, ... 174

CHAPTER VII.

A Dispute with my Uncle and other Jews, who visited me in the Prison of Kiev, as to whether the Messiah has already come, and if Jesus be He; An Attempt on my Life by the Prisoners, ... 179

CHAPTER VIII.

How my Sufferings awakened the Pity of some of the Jews, who sought to obtain my Release; Persecution by my Uncle; Fatiguing March from Kiev; Peculiar Meeting with a former Fellow-Student of a Rabbinical College; Strange Russian Custom for assisting the Dead to enter Heaven; Imprisonment of a Jewish Family on account of the Baptism of one of its Members; Russian Proverbs, ... 191

CHAPTER IX.

Prisoner conducted from Kaselitz to Tchernigov; Five Days of Proclaiming the Gospel in the Prison of Tchernigov; One who had been Imprisoned for Twelve Years without being brought to Trial; The Prison of Homel, and my Visitors; Meeting with my aged Mother and other Relations; Arrival in Mohilev, the Capital of my Native Province; Extract from the *Free Church Record*, ... 196

CHAPTER X.

The Kindness of Pastor Bush, and his Activity for my Liberation; Removal from Prison during the Night, conducted to Bichov; The Wrath of the Jews, and the Burning of my Bible; Second Meeting with my Mother; The Jews resolve to place me in the Russian Army, they do not Succeed; Removal from Bichov, and Meeting with a Russian Priest, to whom I addressed myself for Help; The Consequences, ... 201

CHAPTER XI.

Heavy Fetters, and my Feelings when I was bound in them; Address to Jewish Women, and the Result; A Happy Day of Proclaiming the Gospel to many Jews in the Inn, and in the House of the Rabbi; Removal from Luravits to an Inn on the Highway, where a Conference was held; The Jews divided; One Party about to Drown me in the River Dnieper, when the others came to my Rescue, ... 207

CHAPTER XII.

My Case taken up by Jews in all parts of the Province; Addressing a large Assembly of Jews, who were then divided in their Opinions concerning me; A General Council is held; Resolution to Place me in the Russian Army; The Jews bribe the Vice-Governor, and I am Accepted; My Struggle with the Officers concerning the Oath; Start for Headquarters with a body of raw Recruits, ... 212

CHAPTER XIII.

Description of Barracks in Gomel; How I was appreciated by my Superiors and Fellow-Soldiers; Visited by my Mother and other Relatives; My peculiar kind of Preaching to the Jews in Gomel; Expecting daily to be released from the Army; Extract from the *Free Church Record*; Transferred to the 24th Regiment of Infantry; My attending the full Curriculum of the Military Medical College; Appointed as Medical Officer in the Military Hospital; My Mission Work in Warsaw; My Military Uniform a Protection from the Wrath of the Jews, when I spoke to them of Jesus, ... 216

CHAPTER XIV.

The Nature of my first Journey from Warsaw to my Native Place; A Conditional Invitation from a Cousin of mine; What became of the Money sent from Scotland to buy me out of the Army; Second Journey to my Native Place; The Illness of my Mother; My earnest Conversation with her, and the Result; My Return to Warsaw, and Transfer to St. Petersburg; My Exchanging Words with the Emperor Alexander II. . 223

CHAPTER XV.

The First-fruit of my Work in St. Petersburg; The Baptism of Mr. Kukurizkin, a Jew of the Sect called Karaites; My Happiness in being about the Business of my Heavenly Father; Circle of Christian Friends in St. Petersburg, and Bible-classes in Count Korff's; The Secretary of the London Jewish Missionary Society in St. Petersburg, and my coming in contact with that Society; Letters from Rev. A. Tomory concerning the Free Church of Scotland and the Episcopal Church; My Studies in Theology, ... 228

CHAPTER XVI.

Appointment as Jewish Missionary; First Visit to Scotland; Letter from Rev. J. G. Cunningham; Transferred from London to Bucharest; My First Mission Journeys in Roumania; Preaching the Gospel in a peculiar way to Thousands of Jews; My Winter Work in Bucharest; the Present Jewish Ceremony of the Passover Nights as a Christian Symbol; Letter from the Principal of the Hebrew Missionary College, . . 235

CHAPTER XVII.

My Second and Third Missionary Journeys in Roumania; My Return to London; Correspondence with the Jewish Mission Committee of the Free Church of Scotland; My Second Visit to Scotland, . . . 243

CHAPTER XVIII.

Appointed by the Free Church of Scotland to visit Roumania; Invitation from W. Henderson, Esq., to visit Aberdeen; Letters of Congratulation upon my Appointment from Rev. W. Wingate, Rev. Dr. Stern, Rev. J.

CONTENTS.

B. Barraclough, Assistant-Secretary of the London Jewish Mission Society, and from Rev. J. G. Cunningham; My Visits to Greenock and to Leith; Letter from Rev. J. Thomson; Starting for Roumania; Address to the Jews in Breslau; Arrival in Jassy, ... 251

CHAPTER XIX.

Commencement of Mission Work in Jassy; Evening Religious Discourses—first in Mr. Folticineano's house, then in my own; the Mission Room; the Evening Bible-Class; Saturday Lectures; My Report to the General Assembly of 1881; Rev. D. Edward visits Jassy; His Report to the Committee, and subsequent Letter to Me, ... 256

CHAPTER XX.

Circular to the Learned Jews and Christians concerning the Jewish Question; Answers to My Circular from Dr. Fürst, Dr. Paulus Cassel, Mr. Butynski, of Russia, and Professor Dr. Delitzsch, ... 263

CHAPTER XXI.

The Journal "Eintracht"; Interview on the way to Great Britain with Rev. D. Edward, Professor Paulus Cassel, and other Friends, concerning the Journals, "Eintracht" and "Concordia"; Arrival in London; Consultation with My Friends, Dr. Benoly and Dr. Koppel; Arrival in Edinburgh; Resolution of the Jewish Mission Committee; My Return to Jassy postponed; Pleasant and Profitable Christian Fellowship with the Professor, with My Fellow Students in the New College in Edinburgh, and with Christian Friends in all parts of the Country; Preparation for my Return to Roumania; A Word in Conclusion, ... 272

Part I.

THE MODERN HEBREW;

OR,

THE TALMUDIST AND CABALIST.

AN ACCOUNT OF THE TRADITIONS, CUSTOMS, MANNERS, AND
CEREMONIES OF THE JEWS IN GENERAL, AND OF RUSSIAN
AND POLISH JEWS IN PARTICULAR, TOGETHER
WITH THE AUTHOR'S EARLY LIFE.

CHAPTER I.

MY BIRTHPLACE, MY PARENTS, AND MY CHILDHOOD.

MY birthplace was a beautiful country-seat near the River Dnieper, in a part of the flat tract of West European Russia, in the province of Mohilev.

This Russian province lies between 52° 5′ and 55° 10′ N. latitude, and 28° 50′ and 32° 40′ E. longitude. It contains no mountains; the surface is in general dry, and the soil productive; the climate also is dry and cold. The chief occupations of the inhabitants are agriculture and the rearing of cattle. The wealth of the province is its forests; very large quantities of masts and other timber are floated every spring down the rivers as far as the ports of the Black Sea. The commerce consists of the exportation of corn, flour, flax, hemp, linseed, timber, cattle, wool, tallow, hides, honey, wax, &c., and the most of the business is in the hands of the Jews. The inhabitants are famed for their activity and industry; and from its great natural advantages, Mohilev is considered one of the richest of the Russian provinces.

My parents were a pious, though bigoted Jewish couple, and their chief delight was to train up their children in the religion of their forefathers. I was the youngest son, and the pet of the family. Very early I manifested a strong predilection for Hebrew and for rabbinical literature; and my mother, anxious that I should occupy a high position in the synagogue, spared no pains to procure for me the very best education, in order that I might be fitted for the important position of a rabbi.

The first thing I can remember, and that only as a dream, is the death of my father, when I was not quite four years old. But I have a distinct remembrance of what occurred after that age. Regularly every morning, as soon as I was washed and dressed, my nurse used to take me to my mother, who was seated in her arm-chair, and after the usual morning kiss, I folded my hands, and my mother prayed with me in Hebrew. She would then take me in her arms, kiss me, and carry me to the table where my brother and sisters were assembled. A piece of bread was then placed in my hand, and in a loud voice I pronounced the following blessing in Hebrew: "Blessed art Thou, O Jehovah, our God, King of the Universe, who bringest forth bread from the earth." Then all present would say, "Amen." The meal concluded, I was taught in the Aramean language, to say: "Praised be the merciful One, the Lord and King of this food." In the evening, before I was put to bed, my mother again prayed with me, in Hebrew, concluding with the words: "Into Thy hands, O Lord, I commit my spirit, while I sleep, even until I awake, for Thou, God, art my Protector, in whom I can trust."

At the age of four and a-half years I had a tutor, who instructed me in the Hebrew language. In the space of six months I could read Hebrew fluently : and by the time I was six years old, I had studied the five books of Moses, with the commentary of Rashi.

My tutor, though a very able young man, who took great interest in my studies, did not succeed in gaining my respect; on the contrary, I took great liberties with him, calling him every day by some fresh name, but most frequently " Stupid Moses." This was not praiseworthy, but I think my family encouraged me in this disrespectful conduct by their making too much of me ; every word I uttered was received by them with great applause.

At length my uncle, who visited us about this time, strongly advised my mother to send me to school, before I should be spoiled.

When I became aware of the subject of their conversation, I took a lively part in it, as I was generally allowed to do in most conversations, and I expressed great pleasure at the idea of being amongst other boys, and having a clever teacher who could answer all my questions. But my ideas of a school were quite different from the reality, which I experienced afterwards. Could I have foreseen what it would be, I certainly would not have insisted upon my mother listening to my uncle's advice. She was unwilling to send me to town, but I urged her to do so as soon as possible. I was soon to regret it.

CHAPTER II.

MY FIRST BOARDING-SCHOOL, AND A GLIMPSE AT SOME JEWISH SUPERSTITIONS.

VERY unwillingly my mother went to town to make arrangements for my going to school. She did it more for the sake of gratifying my wishes, than because of my uncle's advice. At my urgent request, I was soon placed in the house of a Jewish teacher who had a private school. His name was Levi. He was a good-natured man, and I might have been very comfortable there but for Rachel, his wife, who was of a very mean disposition. She was the ruler of the house and of everything else. Levi, on the contrary, was weak, and easily influenced by her to do wrong. They had several children of their own, whom they loved very much; and whenever any of my family brought me good things, as cakes, toys, &c., Rachel would take them from me and give them to her own children. When her husband expostulated with her, she would say, " You spoil the child, you do not know how to train children, he was brought here because he had too much at home; besides, these things are not good for him, children must never have too much."

My family frequently visited me, and never failed

to bring me some new thing; but they never inquired how I was treated, taking it for granted that all was right, my mother having chosen this school in preference to a public one, where one child would be easily overlooked amongst the many. I never told that I did not get their presents, for the following reason:— One day when I was bold enough to say that I should tell my mother and sisters that I never had the things they brought for me, Rachel tried to persuade me that the devil would catch me if I did anything so naughty as to report what was done at school. I contradicted her stoutly, saying that my mother had told me that angels watch over children, and where angels are, devils have no power. "Well," answered she, "be naughty, and you will see; I shall go and call him." She then left the room, and in a few minutes a figure appeared with a large black head and a frightfully hideous face, at which I was terribly frightened, as any boy of only six years would be. I ran to Levi, who took me in his arms, and said, "Do not be afraid, the devil only takes naughty children; but if you will be a good boy, and not repeat what is going on in this house, he will not have any power over you." I believed him, and therefore I never told how I was wronged.

The next day, when my school-fellows arrived, I advised them never to be naughty boys, for yesterday I had been naughty, and a black devil came in and would surely have taken me if Levi had not protected me. I told them I had been in terror all night long, and had dreamt of demons, and that I would rather go home than remain there, where they were. "But why do you not ask your mother to take you home?"

inquired one of my companions. "Oh, I must not do that, for the black demon would fetch me before I could get home; Levi said so, and when his wife came in again after the demon was gone, she corroborated what he told me. But I will tell you what we will do," continued I to my fellow-scholars, who were looking very pitifully at me, "we will ask God to let our teacher die, and to give us a better one, for my mother says that God loves children, and hears them when they ask Him anything."

But another boy replied that his father had told him that it was not good to pray for a bad emperor to die, because a worse one might succeed him, and it would be the same with a teacher. "Besides, Levi was not so bad as Jacob Talien, who not only takes the children's money from them, but also beats them to death, as he did my brother."

"Do all the children die who attend Jacob Talien's school?" asked I.

"I do not know if he beats other children so severely."

"But your brother was, perhaps, a very naughty boy," said I.

"Oh! no," replied he, "my brother was a very good boy, but my father and my mother say he beat him because he was not expecting to receive any payment for him."

"But was it not wicked of your father and mother not to pay the teacher?"

"Oh! no," replied the boy, "he had been paid beforehand, for when Jacob wished his daughter to marry, he borrowed money from my father, and promised to instruct his children in return for it. But after my brother died, my father would not send me to his school, lest he should kill me too; nor would he advise any one to send children there."

I then changed the conversation, and asked if any of them had ever seen a demon. "No," was the general reply. One boy then related how his father was sitting alone in his shop late one Saturday night (a night on which, according to Jewish tradition, the demons go about the streets), when a man came in and bought a piece of cloth and paid a good price for it. His father put the money into his pocket, and went home, rejoicing that he had commenced the week so well (it is usual amongst the Jews to consider a good payment on Saturday night as a precursor of a good week); but what was his surprise and consternation in the morning to find coals instead of money in his pocket, and when he returned to the shop, the piece of cloth had not been removed from the place where it had lain for a long time.

Another boy told how, one Wednesday night (also a demon's night, according to Jewish tradition), as his father was going alone past a ruined castle, he saw some demons dancing there, and they called to him, "Berl, come and dance with us!" but taking hold of the fringes on the border of his garments, he repeated the 24th verse of Deut. v.: "Hear, O Israel, Jehovah is our God; Jehovah is one;" and immediately the demons disappeared.*

* I should here observe that every male of the Jewish nation is obliged to have a garment with fringes at the four corners of it, as is commanded in Numbers xv. 37 : "And the Lord spake unto Moses, saying, Speak unto the children of Israel, and bid them that

Another boy said, his father died through a similar occurrence. The demons called him to dance with them, and, in his fright, he forgot to take the fringes in his hand, and to repeat the words, "Hear, O Israel," &c.; so the demons ran after him, seized him, and took him into the ruins, and made him dance with them the whole night, and the next day he died.

These conversations only served to increase my terror and fear of demons, and instead of my usual liveliness I became depressed and unhappy. When my mother or sisters came to see me, they did not notice this, because the joy of seeing them brought back all my brightness. One day, however, my mother, having to leave home for some weeks, came

---

they make them fringes in the borders of their garments throughout their generations, and that they put upon the fringe of the borders a ribbon of blue: and it shall be unto you for a fringe, that ye may look upon it, and remember all the commandments of the Lord and do them; and that ye seek not after your own eyes, after which ye used to go a whoring: that ye may remember, and do all my commandments, and be holy unto your God. I am the Lord your God." This garment is made of two square pieces, with two long slips like straps joined to them, in order that one of the said square pieces may hang down in front, upon the breast, and the other behind. At the extremity of the four corners the fringes are fastened by means of five knots, which knots, with the eight threads of each fringe, make thirteen; and the numerical letters of the Hebrew word *Zittis* amount to six hundred, which, added together, make the number of six hundred and thirteen, which is exactly the number of precepts contained in the law. This garment is called the small veil, which every Jew of the male sex, of whatever condition, is obliged to wear continually. Besides the small veil, they have, when at morning prayers in the synagogue, the large veil with the fringes, which is put on over their garments.

in the morning early to take leave of me. She found me still asleep in bed, but the sight of my pale face and skeleton-like body so alarmed her that she fainted. A doctor was immediately called, who soon restored her, and as soon as she was better she took me home with her. Now she inquired the cause of my having become so thin, but I only replied that I must not tell anything that had been going on at school, for the black demon would fetch me. When she asked what I meant, I replied, "I have seen a demon in Levi's house, and he was going to take me with him, unless I promised not to be a naughty boy any more, nor to say what passed at the school." I was frightened at everything, and as soon as it was dark I was afraid of demons, and became very nervous. Several doctors were called in, but they could not cure me, and my mother was advised to take me to the rabbi. The rabbi here mentioned is not the usual rabbi who is in every town, but one who is supposed by the Jews to have power to command even God. He is also supposed to be able to cure all diseases, and especially to cast out devils, or to cure one who is afraid of them.

It happened that such a rabbi passed through our neighbourhood, and my mother took me to him. He laid his hand upon my head and blessed me, and said, "Child, do not be afraid, the demon will not come to frighten you any more; take this silver piece of money, and wear it on your neck in remembrance of my promise." My faith in the rabbi was such that I then resolved that as soon as I was confirmed, which would be at the age of thirteen, I would go to him and become his disciple.

CHAPTER III.

MY HIGHLY ESTEEMED TUTOR. THIRTEEN ARTICLES OF THE JEWISH FAITH, AND A SPECIMEN OF THE MOST IMPORTANT DAILY PRAYERS.

MY mother determined not to send me to a town school again, but to engage a tutor for me at home, and such an one as would be able to win my respect by his ability and readiness to answer my endless questions; for I never would allow anything to pass without learning its meaning.

After a few weeks of inquiry, my mother chose a young man, named Judah, about twenty-five years of age; he was the son of a rabbi, and himself a candidate for that office. When my mother introduced him to me, and told me he was the son of Rabbi Abraham, and that he himself would be a rabbi as soon as he gets a congregation, I exclaimed: "Oh, how nice to have a tutor, who will soon sit upon the rabbinical chair! But how long will he have to wait until a town be built for his congregation?"

I began to take such liberties with him that my mother feared I should respect him no more than my former tutor, Moses; but Judah was clever enough to know how to win me. The following morning, as soon as I rose and called for water, according to the Jewish custom of pouring water three times over each hand, Judah entered my room, accompanied by a servant with a jug of water and a basin. After the servant had poured water on my hands, Rabbi Judah asked me to repeat after him the following words: "Blessed art Thou, O Jehovah, our God, King of the Universe, who hath sanctified us with His commandments, and commanded us to cleanse our hands." After the pronouncing of the blessing the servant was going to wash me, but I stopped her, and turning to my tutor, I asked him, "Are you going to be a rabbi, Judah? Then please tell me the reason why we pour water three times over each hand, as soon as we rise?" He immediately replied: "Because sleep is an emblem of death, and uncleanness rests on us during sleep; but it departs from us as soon as we rise, and remains only on the hands; therefore we pour water three times over them, to cleanse them, before we touch anything." I was very pleased with this explanation. I thanked him and said, "Rabbi Judah, I hope you will answer everything I am going to ask you about, for I see you are very clever, and there are so many things which I wish explained to me. My first tutor, the stupid Moses, could not explain anything to me, and Levi, the tutor in the town, where the demon was, was too proud to answer children; he used to say, 'Oh, you will understand when you grow up.'" "With God's help, I will answer you everything you ask me," replied my tutor.

The servant then completed my toilet and took me into the school room, where Rabbi Judah awaited me. As soon as I entered he took the fringes of my garment and put them into my hand, and I said, "Blessed art Thou, O Jehovah, our God, King of the Universe, who hath sanctified us with His commandments, and commanded us the commandment of the fringes." Then he opened the Prayer-book, and I read the following prayers: " Blessed art Thou, Jehovah, our God, King of the Universe, who hast formed man with wisdom, and hast created in him holes, pipes, sinews, veins, and joints. It is certain, and known before the throne of Thy glory, that if but one of them were opened or one of them stopped, it would be impossible for mankind to subsist or to stand before Thee. Blessed are Thou, O Jehovah; the healer of all flesh, and wonderful in works."

Then I gave thanks to God for restoring my soul after sleep, in these words : " My God, the soul Thou hast given me is clean ; Thou hast created, and Thou hast formed it, and Thou hast breathed it into me, and Thou dost carefully preserve it within me, and Thou wilt hereafter take it from me, and restore it unto me again in future time ; all the time that the soul continues within me I do acknowledge Thee, O Lord my God, and the God of our fathers, the Governor of all works, and Lord of all souls. Blessed art Thou, O God! the restorer of the soul to the carcases of the dead."

My tutor then accompanied me into the dining room, to my mother, and, after the morning kiss, she asked me how I liked my tutor. I praised him very highly. We then seated ourselves at the table where the rest of the family were assembled, and after taking my coffee without bread (for, from the age of seven years, I was accustomed not to eat anything until I had said my morning prayers, as is usual with the Jews, the children commencing this custom at various ages, not later than thirteen years), I returned with Rabbi Judah to the schoolroom, and read the morning prayers according to the form of the synagogue worship; for those who do not live near a synagogue, or who have no time to attend it, must worship at home three times every day—morning, noon, and night.

It is usual, at the conclusion of the morning prayers, to repeat the thirteen "Fundamental Articles of the Jewish Faith," as follows :—

"I. I believe, with a perfect faith, that God (blessed be His name) is the Creator and Governor of all created things, and that He alone has made, and ever will make, every production.

"II. I believe, with a perfect faith, that the Creator (blessed be His name) is one God; and that there is no unity whatever like unto His; and that He alone is our God, who was, who is, and who will be eternally.

"III. I believe, with a perfect faith, that the Creator (blessed be His name) is incorporeal; that He is not subject to any of the changes incident to matter; and that He has not any similitude whatever.

"IV. I believe, with a perfect faith, that the Creator (blessed be His name) is both the first and the last of all things.

"V. I believe, with a perfect faith, that to the Creator (blessed be His name), yea, to Him only, is it proper to address our prayers, and that it is not proper to pray to any other being.

"VI. I believe, with a perfect faith, that all the words of the prophets are true.

"VII. I believe, with a perfect faith, that the prophecy of Moses, our instructor (may his soul rest in peace), was true prophecy, and that he excelled all the sages who preceded him, or who may succeed him.

"VIII. I believe, with a perfect faith, that the law which we now have in our possession, is the same law which was given to Moses, our instructor (may his soul rest in peace).

"IX. I believe, with a perfect faith, that this law will never be changed, and that the Creator (blessed be His name) will never give us any other law.

"X. I believe, with a perfect faith, that the Creator (blessed be His name) knoweth all the actions and thoughts of man, as it is said, 'He fashioneth all their hearts, and is fully acquainted with all their works.'

"XI. I believe, with a perfect faith, that the Creator (blessed be His name) rewards those who observe His commandments, and punishes those who transgress them.

"XII. I believe, with a perfect faith, that the Messiah will come; and although His coming be delayed, I will still, in daily hope, patiently await His appearance.

"XIII. I believe, with a perfect faith, that there will be a resurrection of the dead, at the time when it shall please the Creator (blessed and exalted be His name for ever and ever)."

The most solemn parts of the Jewish prayers are those which are called *Kiriath Shemah*, and *Shemoneh*

Esreh. The first consists of three portions of Scripture; the first portion of which is taken from Deut. vi. 4-10, the second from Deut. xi. 13-22 and the third from Num. xv. 37 to the end of the chapter. These three portions put together are called *Shemah*, because in the Hebrew Bible the first of them begins with the word *Shemah*—i.e., "hear!" and *Kiriath Shemah* means the reading of the *Shemah.* According to Deut. vi. 7 and xi. 19, the Jews are expressly bound to read it every morning and night.

On inquiring of my tutor what was the meaning of the reading or the repeating of the Shemah, he explained that God had arranged it in order that the Jews might preserve the true religion amongst themselves, in making confession twice every day of the unity of God, and of the duties which they owe to Him.

The other is called *Shemoneh Esreh*—i.e., the eighteen prayers. Here again arose the question, "Why is it called the eighteen prayers, when there are nineteen?" My tutor replied, "By Ezra and the men of the great synagogue, eighteen prayers were composed and instituted; but in the days of Rabbi Gamaliel (who lived a little before the destruction of the second temple), the heretics and apostates having become very troublesome and painful to them, even as thorns in the side, by endeavouring to seduce them from the true religion, and perceiving that this was an essential of the first magnitude in the necessary concerns of mankind, the said Rabbi Gamaliel and his sanhedrim unanimously agreed to compose another prayer, which should contain a request to the Almighty to annihilate the heretics, and they placed it amongst the above eighteen prayers; so that, though there are now nineteen prayers, the portion is still called *Shemoneh Esreh,* the first name which was given by Ezra and the Great Synagogue."

I was quite delighted with these explanations, and in the course of a short time I became so fond of my tutor, that I could not endure to be from his side for a moment; he remained with me until my tenth year.

CHAPTER IV.

THE TALMUD AND ITS ORIGIN.

OUR chief daily study was the Talmud. It is a general impression among Christians that the Talmud includes all the Jewish writers. I have been frequently asked by Christian friends to tell them what the Talmud is, and some readers of this book, when they see the Talmud mentioned, will naturally ask the same question; therefore I deem it necessary to devote a chapter to this subject.

The Talmud contains the fundamental code of the Jewish civil and canonical law. It consists of two parts — the *Mishna,* which is the text, and the *Gemara,* by which some understand a commentary on the Mishna, or a discussion, and others suppose it a supplement or completion.

According to the tradition of the Jews, all the precepts of the law given to Moses were accompanied by an interpretation. God first dictated the text, and gave him an explanation of everything comprehended in it. The text, which is the five books of Moses, was commanded to be put into writing, and the explanation to be committed to memory and to be communicated to that generation, and afterwards transmitted to posterity by word of mouth only. Hence the former is called the written law, and the latter the oral law.

When Moses came down from the Mount, he delivered both these laws to the people, and it was repeated to them several times by Aaron and his sons, and by the seventy elders, so that they all had it firmly fixed in their memories. Towards the end of Moses' life, he repeated and explained the written and the oral law to Joshua, his successor, who was charged with the transmission of it to the next generation. Joshua transmitted it to the elders, who survived him and delivered it to the Prophets; and it was handed down from one prophet to another until it was given to the Great Synagogue, which consisted of Haggai, Zechariah, Malachi, Ezra the Scribe, Nehemiah, Zerrubbabel, and others, amongst the most eminent and leading men of the Jewish nation, who followed the example of those in former ages, in inquiring into the meaning of the law, in making decrees and appointing constitutions. The last of this venerable assembly was Simon the Just, who then filled the office of High Priest, and who was the first of the wise men that are mentioned in the Mishna. After him followed a regular succession, which terminated with Rabbi Jehuda *Hakkodesh*, or the "holy," a man of eminent talent and virtue. He lived in the second century A.D.; and from the time of Moses to his own days no part of the oral law had ever been committed to writing for public perusal.

In every generation the president of the sanhedrim, or the prophet of his age, for his own private use, wrote notes of the traditions which he had heard from his teachers; but he taught in public only by word of mouth. Thus things proceeded till the days of Rabbi Jehuda. This venerable rabbi observed that the students of the law were gradually diminishing, that difficulties and distress were multiplying, that the kingdom of impiety was increasing in strength and extending itself over the world, and that the people of Israel were driven to the ends of the earth; and fearing lest under these circumstances the traditions would be forgotten and lost, he collected them all, and arranged them under distinct heads, and formed them into a methodical code of traditional law. This code, called Mishna, was compiled by Rabbi Jehuda about 180 A.D. Copies were speedily multiplied and circulated, and the Jews at large received it with the highest veneration.

The Mishna is written in a very concise style, in the Aramaic language, and is divided into six sections.

Section I., entitled "Zerohim," *i.e.*, "seeds," contains eleven books, treating of those laws which concern agriculture. The first book of this section— "Berachath," *i.e.*, "blessings"—contains forms of prayers and thanksgivings for the fruits of the earth, and all other benefits of what nature soever, together with the circumstances of time and place in which they are to be used; and all these are ordered that the Jews may not lawfully make use of, or enjoy, these creatures without previous thanksgiving.

Section II., entitled, "Moed," *i.e.*, "festivals," so called because it contains laws concerning festivals and days of solemn observation. It comprises twelve books.

Section III., "Noeshem," *i.e.*, "woman," contains seven books, which treat of the laws of marriages, divorces, cases of jealousy, and other matters concerning woman.

Section IV., "Nyzikin," *i.e.*, "damage" or "injuries," includes a great part of the civil and criminal law; it comprises eight books. The seventh, entitled "Aboth," *i.e.*, "fathers," or "sentences of the fathers," contains some of the sublimest diction known in the history of religious philosophy.

Section V., "Kœdoshim," *i.e.*, "holy things," contains eleven books, in which the laws of all religious performances whatsoever are treated.

Section VI., "Taharoth," *i.e.*, "purifications," comprises twelve books, which treat of the general laws concerning pollutions and purifications.

About a century after the Mishna was compiled, Rabbi Jochanan, president of the Jewish Academy at Tiberias, collected various opinions of learned men, who were employed in explaining the difficulties of the Mishna, and compiled the Gemara, or Commentary, which, added to the text of the Mishna, forms what is denominated the Jerusalem Talmud. It is written in what may be called the East Aramæan language.

The Jews in Chaldea, who were greater in number and wealth, were not satisfied with this production, they did not accept this commentary; the chief study in all their schools and colleges was the Mishna, and the doctors, for several generations, made it their text-book, investigating its latent meaning and delivering interpretations, each according to the degree of his knowledge and understanding. The expositions of some of these doctors were at variance with the conclusions of others, so that in process of time very different and contradictory opinions were promulgated respecting many of the Mishna maxims and ordinances.

These researches and discussions were continued to the days of Rabina and Rabbi Ashe. Rabbi Ashe undertook, A.D. 365, to make a collection of these various interpretations of the Mishna, which bears the name of the Babylonian Gemara, and, together with the Mishna, formed the Babylonian Talmud. Rabbi Ashe died A.D. 427, and his coadjutors and their successors finally completed this codex towards the end of the fifth century.

When the Talmud was completed, the Doctors made it their sole object to understand and explain what was contained in it, without presuming to add anything to it, or to take anything from it; and although many commentaries have been written to explain it, all of which are highly esteemed by the Jews, the Talmud remains as it was about fourteen centuries ago.

The Jews in Russia, Poland, and the East make the Talmud, with its commentaries, their chief study, and every Jew thinks that in studying the Talmud he pleases God. So it was with me. I studied it not only for the sake of knowing it, but also to please God; and so great was my zeal in this respect, that I knew by heart nearly every book of it which I studied.

CHAPTER V.

LEAVE-TAKING OF MY TUTOR ON HIS BEING CALLED TO BE A RABBI, AND THE CONSECRATION OF THE NEW MOON.

RABBI JUDAH, the tutor whom I loved so dearly, and by whom I had been so well instructed in the Talmud and many other things, was called to the office of rabbi in a Jewish congregation, in a town some distance from my home. I was now about ten years of age, and during the three years my tutor had been with me I had become so closely attached to him, that I could not now endure a separation. But his new calling would not allow of his remaining with me; therefore I obtained my mother's permission to accompany him to Teicersk, that I might at least see him seated on the rabbinical chair.

The following day we set out on our journey, and after two days we arrived at our destination.

When about a mile from the town, we were met by a Jewish deputation, who accompanied us to the house of the chief of the synagogue, where a great number of Jews had assembled to salute the new rabbi. This was on Friday, and the next day being the Jewish Sabbath, Rabbi Judah preached in the afternoon, in the synagogue, to a crowded audience.

I was delighted to see such a congregation listening to my tutor, and I felt a longing for the time when I too might speak to such an audience. He preached for more than two hours; then the usual Sabbath afternoon prayers were offered. After the close of the service, he was invited by another ruler of the synagogue to partake of the third meal of the Sabbath. All this time I remained close to my tutor, who never lost sight of me for a moment, but even introduced me to the congregation as his true disciple, and as a future rabbi. It was an intense delight to me to see my tutor so honoured, and I only regretted that I had not esteemed him more during the three years he was under our roof.

The feast which the ruler gave in honour of Rabbi Judah, to which many learned and rich Jews were also invited, lasted until day-break; it was only interrupted by our going to the synagogue as soon as it was dark, to offer the evening prayers. After this, the whole congregation sallied forth into the open air, that they might have a clear view of the moon (it being a custom among the Jews to consecrate the new moon on the first Saturday evening in the month, providing it be then visible; otherwise, the first clear evening afterwards). Rabbi Judah then pronounced the following benediction, in which he was joined by the whole assembly:—

"Blessed art Thou, O Lord our God, King of the Universe, who with His word created the heavens, and with His breath all the host thereof,—a statute and a time He gave unto them, that they should not vary from their orders; they are glad, and they rejoice to obey the will of their Maker; the Maker is true, and all His works are true : and to the moon He said that she shall monthly renew her crown of beauty towards those who are the fruit of the womb; for they hereafter shall be renewed like unto her, to praise their Creator for the glory of His name and kingdom. Blessed art Thou, O Lord! the renewer of the months.'"

Then the whole assembly lifted up their heads towards the moon, and, raising themselves on their toes several times, repeated three times : " As I jump towards Thee, and yet cannot reach to touch Thee, so shall none of mine enemies be able to touch me to harm." Then they said three times : "Fear and dread shall fall upon them; by the greatness of Thine arm they shall become still as a stone; as a stone they shall become still; and by the greatness of Thine arm, dread and fear on them shall fall. David, King of Israel, liveth and subsisteth."

Then they saluted each other with, "Peace be unto you"; and the others responded, "Unto you be peace."

With great enthusiasm they continued : " The voice of my beloved : behold he cometh leaping upon the mountains, skipping upon the hills. My beloved is like a roe or a young hart; behold he standeth behind our wall : he looketh forth at the windows, showing himself through the lattice."

It was taught in the school of Rabbi Ismael, that had the Israelites been allowed thus to reverence the Divine presence of their Father who is in heaven, only once a month, it might suffice them. Abaya saith : "Therefore is it necessary to be said, in an erect posture, 'Who is this coming from the wilderness, leaning on her beloved.' May it be thy pleasure, O God, and the God of our Fathers, to continue to fill up the deficiencies of the moon; and that the light of the moon be as the light of the sun; as her light was during the first six days of the creation, before her diminution; as it is said, 'the two great lights.' Oh, may the verse be fulfilled, 'And they will seek the Lord their God, and David their King!' Amen."

CHAPTER VI.

THE DUTIES OF THE RABBI, AND THE DIVORCE CEREMONY.

THE fortnight spent with my tutor in his new capacity was a time of much greater delight to myself than to him, for he had no rest from the people, who assailed him the whole day with all kinds of questions.

One woman came and inquired what she ought to do with some meat upon which milk had been spilt. Another asked what she should do with some milk into which a drop of blood had fallen. A third came with the gizzard of a chicken in which she had found a piece of a needle, and asked if it was lawful to eat the chicken. These, and many like questions, were put to him by women, and by boys and girls who were sent by their parents. Frequently these children forgot the question, and had to be sent home for it. It greatly amused me to see a boy come and stand before the rabbi with folded hands and uplifted eyes, and when asked what he wanted he would reply, "My mother sent me with a question to the rabbi." "Well, what is it?" "Oh, rabbi, I have forgotten it!" "Then go back and ask what it was." The boy would go perhaps as far as the door, and then return, saying, "Rabbi, I recollect it." "Well?" "Oh, I do not know!"

Very often men would come who had some quarrel in business, that the rabbi might judge between them. On such occasions Rabbi Jehudah would sit very gravely, the men standing before him, stating alternately their grievances. He would then recommend them to be reconciled, rather than be judged by the law of the Talmud. If, however, both or one of them refused to make peace, then he would have recourse to the books of the law, and, if required, witnesses were called in, and a trial commenced. At the conclusion, the rabbi would ask if both parties were satisfied with it; and should either not be content, then he might appeal to the judgment of three rabbis.

Two divorce cases were also brought before him, one of which amused me so much that I will give a description of it. A Jewish couple came, each of them wishing to make it appear that he or she was the party who wished for the divorce. The woman was the first, who said, "Rabbi, we wish to be divorced." On his inquiring for what reason, and what she had against her husband, she replied, "Excuse me, rabbi, I cannot say anything ill of him as long as he is my husband." He then asked the man if he wished to divorce his wife. He replied, "Certainly; for what else are we come here; is it not for that purpose?" "But for what reason?" asked the rabbi. "Oh, rabbi, I need not remind you that according to the law of our wise men (blessed be their memory), every Jew is at liberty to divorce his wife at any time, and for any cause, or for no substantial cause at all; and the husband himself is the sole judge of its sufficiency." "But it is my duty to prevent divorces from taking place on sudden sallies of passion, which might afterwards be regretted," said Rabbi Jehudah. "Rabbi," said the man, "it is not so sudden as you think; we wanted to be divorced long since, but our old rabbi was ill for some weeks, and could not perform our divorce; then, since his death we have waited so many weeks for another rabbi, and now you are going to put difficulties in the way, which our old rabbi never did, for I myself have divorced three wives already, and the last time he said, if all his congregation would do the same, he would have a greater income; and he even asked me when he might expect me again for the same purpose."

My good tutor was astonished to hear his detail, and replied, "I do not want to hear of my predecessor neither am I inclined to divorce people in haste; go home now, and when you have thought the matter over, come again in three days." Neither the man nor his wife could keep their temper longer, and they said they would not leave the house till the divorce were completed. They made so much noise that the good rabbi was compelled to agree to their urgent request. He told them to call in ten men, who must be present, and two witnesses to sign the divorce bill. "Oh, that is right," said the man gladly, and away he went, returning in a short time with the ten men, two witnesses, and also a scribe, who, after he had received the pen from the hand of the husband, wrote the following bill of divorce in Hebrew:—

"On the fifth day of the week, on the —— day of the month ——, in the year —— from the creation

DUTIES OF THE RABBI, AND THE DIVORCE CEREMONY. 31

of the world; according to the computation which we follow here in the city of Teicersk, which is called Zizersk, situated by the sides of the rivers Sos and Prosk, I, Simon, the son of Isaac, surnamed Simsons, and at this time dwelling in the city of Teicersk, which is called Zizersk, which is situated by the sides of the rivers Sos and Prosk—or if I have any other name, or surname, or my parents, or my place, or the place of my parents—by my own free will, without any compulsion, do put away, dismiss, and divorce thee, my wife Jente, the daugher of Chaim, the priest, who at this time resides in the city of Mohilow, called Mohilev, situated by the Rivers Dnieper and Dubrowinka—or if thou hast any other name, or surname, or thy parents, or thy place, or the place of thy parents—who wast heretofore my wife, but now I put thee away, dismiss, and divorce thee; so that from this time thou art in thine own power, and art at thine own disposal, and mayest be married to any other man, whom thou pleasest, and let no man hinder thee in my name, from this day forward and for ever; and lo, thou art free to any man. Let this be to thee from me a bill of divorce, an instrument of dismission, and a letter of separation, according to the law of Moses and Israel."

David, the son of Moses, witness.

Mordecai, the son of Zachariah, witness.

When this was ready, both parties appeared again before the rabbi, the ten men standing round, and the two witnesses, one on either side, while he proceeded to ascertain whether this act were the result of their own free choice. After obtaining satisfaction on this point, and seeing the bill duly executed and signed by the witnesses, he directed the man to deliver it to the woman, who stood with partly folded hands to receive it. The man dropped it between the palms of her hands, saying as he did so, "Behold, this is thy bill of divorce, and thou art herewith divorced from me, and art free to any other man."

When this ceremony was over, I went up to the woman and asked her, "Now, good soul, as long as that man was your husband, you refused to say anything against him, but now you can tell your reason for wishing to be divorced." She replied, "Oh, dear boy, you wish to know everything; you will grow old too soon, but that man is now a stranger to me, and I do not like to speak against strangers." "You are a clever wicked little woman," said I, turning away from her.

CHAPTER VII.

THE CEREMONY OF CIRCUMCISION AND REDEMPTION OF THE FIRST-BORN.

AFTER my fortnight's stay with my late tutor, I accompanied my mother and brother to Mohilew, where the latter resided. We found, on our arrival, that my brother's wife expected soon the birth of her first-born. The necessary preparations for such an important occasion were soon made by my brother, and among others I may mention that all round the walls of his wife's room he described circles with a piece of chalk; and over the windows, doors, and fireplace were put papers, on which were written in Hebrew the 121st Psalm, and the names of angels which are supposed to defend the child from the injuries of Lileth, who is said to have been transformed into a female demon, and takes delight in debilitating and destroying young infants. By such methods the room was believed to be sufficiently protected against the intrusion of evil spirits.

Before the birth of the child, my brother and I went to the synagogue, where ten men were called in, and after reading the 20th, 38th, 92nd, and the 102nd Psalms, a long prayer was offered. We found, on our return to the house, that a son had been born during our absence, and it was a season of great joy to our family.

During the first week many little boys were brought every evening into the chamber, where the mother and child were, and they read the 6th chapter of Deuteronomy from 4th to 10th verse, also some psalms and prayers. The children's pockets were then filled with good things, and money was given to their leader, the assistant teacher. They then went away rejoicing, and our family felt secure from any evil spirit entering that night into this chamber.

The next thing to be considered was the preparations for the solemn feast of circumcising the child. Dainties of all kinds were procured — fish, flesh, fowl, and abundance of wines. Cards of invitation were printed.

On the seventh night, ten learned Jews were invited, who passed the night in reading the Talmud and the holy book of the Zohar, and in offering prayers; this is done from the belief that on this night both mother and son are in more than common danger of some misfortune by evil spirits.

On the eighth day, we went to the synagogue, where many candles were lighted for the occasion, and after the morning prayers the preparations for the ceremony were conducted in the most splendid style. In the first place, a beautiful chair with two seats, adorned with a costly covering and silken cushions, was placed near the chest in which the peculiarly esteemed and sacred book of the law of Moses was deposited. Then my brother, who was himself the Baal-Berith—*i.e.*, master of the circumcision—approached the chair; next to him stood the circumciser, who could be distinguished from the others by his very long and sharp thumb-nails, with which both hands are adorned, as a badge of his profession; and the whole congregation stood around. The circumciser then sang several songs in Hebrew, after which the infant, lying on a costly cushion, was brought to the door of the synagogue by a large company of females, one of whom placed it in the arms of a young girl, who presented it to me as I met her at the door, with an attendant bearing a lighted taper. Having received the child, I turned with my face towards the assembly, who then shouted "BARUCH HABBA," *i.e.*, "Blessed is he that cometh!" This "Baruch Habba" was meant for the child coming to enter into the community of Israel, and also for Elijah, the prophet, who is supposed by the Jews to enter the room with the infant, and to sit in the vacant seat of the double chair, in order to observe whether the covenant of circumcision be duly administered. For this reason this chair is called Elijah's chair. I then advanced a few steps with the child in my arms, preceded by two officers of the synagogue bearing lighted tapers; it was then taken from me and handed from one to another until it reached the place where Elijah's chair stood. I then again received it into my arms and delivered it to my brother, who laid it on the chair. The circumciser then chanted with a loud voice the following: "This is the chair of the Prophet Elijah, the angel of the covenant; behold, it is sent for thee, stand at my right hand and help me."

The rabbi then took the child from the chair, and my brother taking the vacant seat, the child was laid upon his knees; and during the act of circumcision the circumciser said with a loud voice: "Blessed art Thou, O Lord our God, King of the Universe, who hast sanctified us with Thy commandments, and commanded us to observe the rite of circumcision." When the rite was completed, he continued, "Blessed art Thou, O Lord our God, King of the Universe, who hast sanctified us with Thy commandments, and commanded us to introduce him into the covenant of our Father Abraham."

The congregation then said: "As he is introduced into the covenant, so may he be initiated into the law, the nuptial canopy, and good works."

My brother then rose from his seat with the child, and placed it in the arms of the rabbi. The circumciser then took into his hand a silver cup filled with wine, and pronounced the following benediction: "Blessed art Thou, O Lord our God, King of the Universe! the Creator of the fruit of the vine. Blessed art Thou, O Lord our God! who hath sanctified his beloved from the womb, and ordained an ordinance for his kindred, and sealed his descendants with the mark of His holy covenant; therefore, for the merits of this, O living God, our rock and inheritance! command the deliverance of the beloved of our kindred from the pit, for the sake of the covenant which He hath put in our flesh. Blessed art Thou, O Lord, the Maker of the covenant!" Then followed this prayer for the child: "Our God, and the God of our fathers! preserve this child to his father and mother, and his name shall be called in Israel, Joel, the son of Clement. Let the father rejoice in those that proceed from his loins, and the woman be glad in the fruit of her womb ; as it is said, 'Thy father and thy mother shall rejoice, and they who begat thee shall be glad' (Prov. xxiii. 25). It is also said, 'And I passed by thee, and saw thee polluted in thine own blood; and I said unto thee, In thine own blood shalt thou live' (Ezek. xvi. 6). And it is said, 'He hath remembered His covenant for ever, the word which He commanded to a thousand generations; which He covenanted with Abraham, and likewise His oath unto Isaac; and He confirmed the same to Jacob for a statute, to Israel for an everlasting covenant'" (Psalm cv. 8-10).

The congregation here repeated these words: "'O give thanks unto the Lord, for He is good, and His mercy endureth for ever.' Joel, this little one, may God make him great. As he has been entered into the covenant, so may he be initiated into the law, the precepts, the nuptial canopy, and good works."

The consecrated cup was then handed to my brother; then to all the boys in attendance, who drank of it. And the ceremony was concluded by carrying the infant back to its home.*

* This is the usual ceremony of the circumcision of Jewish children, but should it happen that a Gentile wished to be circumcised (a case which never occurs in Russia, as the law of the country does not permit it), he must be also baptised; for, according to the Talmudic law, a Gentile, if he is circumcised and not baptised, cannot be admitted as a member of the Jewish community. The reason of this is, that the Jews are a holy people, and their children being born of holy parents, do not need to be baptised; but a Gentile, who is born of unholy parents, must be purified through baptism. This is done in the following manner: ten men take the Gentile to the usual pool for Jewish purification, he goes into the water and dips himself three times, while the

A large number of the guests who were invited to the ceremony returned with us to the banquet in my brother's house, which lasted the whole day.

The next ceremony which took place, on the thirty-first day after the child was born, was that of the redemption of the first-born, which was performed in the following manner. My brother sent for a priest and some friends. This priest is one who calls himself "cohen"—*i.e.*, priest—and who is supposed to be a descendant of Aaron, but who never pretends to establish this claim by any genealogy. The guests and priest being assembled, my brother placed his little son on a table, and said to the priest, "My wife, who is an Israelitess, has brought me a first-born, but our law which was given to us by God, through Moses (blessed be his memory), assigns him to thee." The priest then asked my brother if he surrendered his son to him. "No," answered he. The priest then asked if he wished to redeem him. "Yes," was the reply of my brother, who then charged the priest to accept the due sum of five shekels, which is about the value of nine shillings and fourpence; and then subjoined this benediction: "Blessed art Thou, O Jehovah, our God, King of the Universe! who hast sanctified us with Thy commandments, and commanded us to perform the redemption of the son. Blessed art Thou, O Jehovah, our God, King of the Universe! who hast preserved us alive, sustained us, and brought us to enjoy this season."

bystanders repeat in Hebrew three times: "Clean! clean! clean!" The same ceremony of baptism is performed by Jewish women for a Gentile woman wishing to become a Jewess.

My brother then produced money to the value of five shekels. The priest took it, and placed it on the head of the child, saying, "This son being a first-born, the blessed God hath commanded us to redeem him, as it is said: 'And those that are to be redeemed, from a month old thou shalt redeem them, according to thine estimation, for the money of five shekels, after the shekel of the sanctuary, which is twenty gerahs.' (Numb. xviii. 16.) 'Whilst thou wast in thy mother's womb, thou wast in the power of thy Father, who is in heaven, and in the power of thy parents; but now thou art in my power, for I am a priest. But thy father and mother are desirous to redeem thee, for thou art a sanctified first-born.'" (Exod. xiii. 2.) He then turned to my brother, saying, "I have received these five shekels from thee for the redemption of this thy son, and behold, he is therewith redeemed, according to the law of Moses and Israel."

A feast followed this ceremony, and the next day my brother accompanied me home to our country seat. Here I found a new tutor had been provided for me; but I did not like him, and therefore I persuaded my mother to send me to school in town, where I could often see my brother's baby-boy, whom I dearly loved. My mother agreed to it, and in a few weeks the necessary arrangements were made.

CHAPTER VIII.

MY ESTABLISHING A SOCIETY FOR THE CLOTHING OF POOR CHILDREN; CONFIRMATION AT THE AGE OF THIRTEEN; AND MY FIRST SERMON IN THE SYNAGOGUE.

AS I said before, I was now ten years of age, and I remained at school in the town where my brother lived, until I was thirteen. I grew up an earnest, thoughtful lad, full of reverence for the creed of my fathers, which I regarded as the only one given by Jehovah to man, and I devoted myself zealously to good works. In the first place, I began to organise a society for clothing the poor children, that they might not be hindered from attending school and the daily prayers in the synagogue. To this end I found it necessary to draw up the following rules:—

I. The society shall be called *Malbish Arumin;* i.e., clothing the naked.

II. The society shall have a president, a vice-president, two secretaries, and a treasurer.

III. The selection of the officials of the society shall be invested in a committee of twelve of the members, who shall be appointed by drawing lots. All the members' names shall be written upon slips, rolled up and put together. The first twelve which are drawn shall be the committee, who shall then choose the president, vice-president, secretaries, and treasurer from the whole of the members, the committee themselves excepted.

IV. Every member of the society who pays his enrolling fee and weekly subscription shall be considered as a member of the committee.

V. Every member of the society shall pay a tax upon every new article of clothing he puts on. This tax shall be fixed by the president or vice-president in a meeting of ten members. The amount of the tax shall be according to the position of the members.

VI. Every Friday two of the members shall call upon all the rest for their weekly subscriptions. All the members shall take their turn, two and two, in collecting.

VII. Any member who absents himself from the general meeting, or who fails to take his turn in collecting, shall pay a fine according to his circumstances. This fine shall be decided by the president or the vice-president, in a meeting of ten members.

VIII. In all decisions the president shall have three votes, and the vice-president shall have two votes. The president and the vice-president shall always have the casting votes.

IX. As the society consists of members who are still under parental control, no member shall be accepted unless he bring a certificate from his parents or his guardians, that they will be responsible for all the expenses.

The society rapidly increased, and at our first annual meeting it numbered three hundred members, and had an income of over eight hundred roubles, which was very carefully expended. This annual meeting was concluded with a feast, the expenses of which were borne by the members, who were required to pay twenty-five kopeks each.

Happy was I when I attained the age of thirteen, at which age I had all the rights of manhood. Amongst the Jews the ceremony of confirmation then takes place. Until then the father, or, if he be not alive, the eldest brother, is liable to Divine and human punishment for the offences of the boy. Therefore, when a boy attains this age, the father declares before the congregation in the synagogue that his son is of age, that he has been instructed in the commandments, is fully acquainted with the decision and customs respecting the Tsitsith and Tephillim, and that he shall be no longer chargeable with the sins of his son; as he is now a Bar Mitsvah, *i.e.*, a son of the commandment, he shall henceforth bear his own sins. As my father was not alive, my brother performed this ceremony.

We went to the synagogue where friends and relatives, who had been invited for the occasion, awaited us. Near the end of the service, the law of Moses was taken out of the ark, and I was called to read in it. My brother stood at my right hand, and my teachers, together with Rabbi Jehuda, my late tutor, who had come from a distance, stood at my left. My mother and sisters, and many female friends and relations, were in the gallery, as it is not lawful in a Jewish synagogue that men and women should be together.

After I had read a portion in the Mosaic law, my

brother, who acted in place of a father to me, gave special thanks to God that he was now relieved and freed from the punishment incurred by me, and he offered prayers on my behalf that I might live for many years, and be eminent for good works.

I then delivered my first sermon, from Deut. vi. 6-8: "And these words, which I command thee this day, shall be in thine heart: And thou shalt teach them diligently unto thy children, and shalt talk of them when thou sittest in thine house, and when thou walkest by the way, and when thou liest down, and when thou risest up. And thou shalt bind them for a sign upon thine hand, and they shall be a frontlet between thine eyes." There was a large and attentive audience, and my instructors were proud of the manner in which their youthful disciple had acquitted himself. A brilliant future was predicted for me by the admiring friends who gathered round my happy mother and relations. All my relatives and friends, who had been invited for the occasion, went with me to my brother's house, where a banquet was prepared.

From this time I was (according to Jewish custom) considered of full age and able to act for myself. I resolved, therefore, to go to the rabbi who had cured me of the fright of the demon, as I related in chap. ii.; and not only so, but being imbued with a deep sense of religion, and elated with the praises of my genius and talents by my relatives and friends, I was fired with an insatiable desire to go to that rabbi and to become his true disciple, and to prosecute with renewed ardour my beloved studies, in the hope of one day occupying a high position in the synagogue.

CHAPTER IX.

A BOY'S EXTRAORDINARY JOURNEY IN ORDER TO VISIT MIRACLE-PERFORMING RABBIS, AND THE DEMON IN A CELLAR.

ON the day after my confirmation, I informed my mother of my resolve to go to the miracle-performing rabbi, and to be his disciple. She, however, refused her consent, saying that I was as yet only a boy, and too young for such an undertaking; and also that the rabbi would not receive me at that age for a disciple; besides he lived too far from my home. "Mother," said I, "you know that since yesterday I am a man, and have all the rights of manhood, and I do not see anything to hinder me from going to Chozimsk, the residence of the rabbi; at least I must go and see him." For several days I conversed with my mother upon this subject, but she would by no means hear of my taking such a journey I therefore wilfully determined to carry out my own plans; and fearing lest my mother should in any way hinder me, I took advantage of her absence for a few days to leave my home, unknown by any one.

I set out on foot to a town about ten miles distant. On my arrival, as I passed along one street, I heard the voices of Jewish children, and entered the house, which consisted of only one room—in fact a wooden hut, the floor of which was covered with mud. A teacher was seated at the head of a table, around which sat also thirteen or fourteen wretched children. The teacher's wife was cooking at the stove, from which poured such volumes of smoke that it was impossible to speak a word, and I left without making the inquiries I had intended. A little further on I met a Jew, who knew me, and asked me where I was going; to which I replied, "I am going to a rabbinical school." "But how is it that you are alone and on foot, instead of driving?" "You have no business to ask questions," was my answer, as I turned away from him. I then went to an inn, where I found a hackney carriage going in the direction of Chozimsk; I paid my fare, and drove away with the six other passengers. After a few days' travelling, and several times changing carriages, we arrived at Chozimsk.

My happiness on arriving was soon to be clouded, for I found that the rabbi, to whom I was so indebted, was dead, and that his son, who had succeeded him, was away from town. I resolved to remain till he should return, and during the interval I made the acqaintance of a pious Jew, called Chaim Moses. His daily occupation was to visit the sick and poor, and I used to accompany him in his visits, when I saw for the first time what misery really is.

One day I went as usual, after my morning prayers and study in the synagogue, to the house of Chaim Moses, that we should make our customary round of visits, but found that he himself was ill. He asked me to go alone to see a poor sick Jew, and carry to him some money for bread and meat. I went, and found at his bedside another Jew, with whom he was having a very hot dispute about miracle-performing rabbis. The one now in question was called Jankel, and the sick man declared that he would rather die than believe in Jankel as a miracle performer; he had not believed in his father, he said, who was a *zadic*—*i.e.*, a righteous man—and how should he believe in his son, whom he knew to be a wicked man? This greatly incensed his visitor, and he exclaimed, "Smerul! you are poor because you did not believe in the old rabbi, and you are now ill because you do not believe in his son, who is his successor."

"O Joseph," said the sick man, "if you only heard what my rabbi said of Jankel, you would not believe in him yourself. He says that he is not a rabbi at all, and that his *neshama*—*i.e.*, soul—is not of the souls of the rabbis."

"But who is your rabbi?" returned Joseph in great wrath.

"Our blessed rabbi says that he is not a holy man."

The noise was so great, and the quarrel so high, that some neighbours came to see what the matter was, and Joseph left the house in a rage. I then took my seat beside the poor man, and tried to quiet him, asking him to have a good rest after his fatiguing talk; but he said he would not rest until he should tell me of this Jankel. "I am," said he, "a *chosid* of Rabbi Moses of Irzitshev; I visit him every year, sometimes even twice or thrice, and am always delighted to see his face, which shines like an angel's; I listen to each word that proceeds from his holy lips, and I often heard him say that even the father of Jankel was not ordained by any ordained rabbi to perform miracles. When I used to return from my holy rabbi, I told the chassidim of our town what I had heard from the holy Rabbi Moses, and as soon as it came to the ears of Jankel he tried to persecute me, and he still tries to do so."

"But why do you live here where all are your enemies?" asked I.

Smerul replied: "Oh, not my will must be done, but the will of the rabbi, and he commanded me to remain in this town, and to bear witness of him even unto death."

I was so moved by these words, that I was for going at once to the town of Rabbi Moses; but the idea came into my mind, Is it possible that a holy rabbi should speak ill of another through envy? instead of saying, like Moses, the true servant of God (in Num. xi. 29), "Would God that all the Lord's people were prophets, and that the Lord would put His spirit upon them."

I resolved not to wait any longer for Rabbi Jankel, but I did not know where to take my journey first, not liking to return home without having discovered what these miracle-performing rabbis were. I therefore returned to Chaim Moses to ask his advice, but could get no help from him, as he was true to all the rabbis, and said they were all holy men. Being thus left to myself, I resolved to visit as many of these rabbis as I could, and at once followed Rabbi Jankel to Czarnigow, where he intended to remain for two or three weeks.

On my arrival there I found all his rooms, as well

as outside his house, crowded with Jews, men, women, and children, waiting for admission to the rabbi, who received them one by one. One of the rabbi's attendants stood at the door; I went up to him and said, "I wish to see the rabbi, for whom I have a letter from Chaim Moses." The man communicated my message, and returned almost immediately to usher me into the rabbi's presence.

He was seated in an arm-chair, dressed in a white silk robe with silver embroidery on the wristbands, collar, and front. I delivered the letter to him, and after reading it, he said he was extremely happy to see one whom his father had cured of the fear of demons, and he inquired if I wished to become his disciple? I answered boldly, "Rabbi, I must know you first." He opened very wide eyes, and looking sharply at me, drew me to his side, saying with a prophetic air, "I see something particular in you, my dear son, you will one day be one of the greatest rabbis, if the *klipa* (*i.e.*, evil spirit) will not take possession of you; but should he do so, you will be a great destroyer of the Jewish synagogue. "Rabbi," said I, "will you permit me to stay some days with you?" "Certainly; and I should be happy if you would stay not only some days, but if you would become my disciple, for I see that your soul comes of the line of the great rabbis; it must, therefore, be watched over, lest the *klipa* take possession of it." I remained with him, and he kept me at his side, and told the people much about my "high soul, and how his father's prayers had once delivered it from the power of the *klipa*, who was getting possession of it." Thus he made use of me to augment his own and his father's power.

One day, whilst sitting as usual with the rabbi, we heard loud cries for help, and several Jews came in saying that there was a demon in David Baruch's cellar, and they begged him to go and cast it out. He refused to go until they paid him eighteen roubles. The sum was immediately paid, whereupon Jankel took his father's stick and proceeded towards David Baruch's house, followed by an eager, curious crowd, anxious to see the miracle about to be performed. We could not enter the cellar for the quantity of stones and turnips which were thrown from it. Jankel called with a loud voice, "Demon, I command thee, in the name of Jehovah, to leave the cellar, and to go to that place where there are no human dwellings." This he repeated several times, but still the stones and turnips were thrown. Jankel was at a loss to know how to proceed. Again he repeated, "In the name of my father, I command thee to leave the cellar," but with no result. Seeing the Rabbi in such distress, I begged him to give me the stick, saying, I would cast out the demon. At first he refused to loose it, but at last he yielded to me. I took it, and called out very loudly, "Know, O man or demon, whichever it may be, if thou wilt not leave the cellar at once, I shall destroy you like the destruction of Jerusalem." After a moment's silence, the shower of stones and turnips at once ceasing, a boy of about ten came from the cellar, whom David Baruch and his wife recognised as their naughty son. Rabbi Jankel said nothing, but taking the stick from my hand, in great agitation he hastened home. The parents would have beaten their boy, but I prevented them by begging them to leave him to me for one hour.

I went with the boy into the house, accompanied by his parents and some friends, and after requesting silence, I began to question the boy as to his reason for playing such a trick. He replied that he had not meant to do so, but was simply hiding in the cellar, as he did not wish to go to school. However, hearing his mother going into the cellar, and fearing lest she might find him and beat him, he began to throw the turnips and stones, in order to frighten her. I then asked why he did not come out of the cellar when the rabbi commanded him, but only when I spoke to him. He answered that there was no fear of the rabbi going into the cellar, but when he heard me threatening destruction, he became frightened lest I should shoot into the cellar with a pistol. "But were you not afraid that the rabbi should destroy you with the words of his mouth?" said I. "Oh no!" was the reply; "I was not afraid of a rabbi who did not know whether a man or a demon was in the cellar."

Rabbi Jankel was so ashamed over this affair, that he was obliged to leave the town at once. He wished me to accompany him, but I said I would have nothing to do with such a miracle-performing rabbi, who asks money for that which he cannot do.

I remained some days longer in Czarnigow, during which time I was invited from house to house by the rich Jews, that they might see the extraordinary boy who had exposed the rabbi. I wished also to convince myself whether these rabbis were real miracle performers, or whether, as they are called by some of the Jews, they were "*betrüger*," or "*betrogene betrüger*,"—*i.e.*, deceivers, or deceiving themselves.

The rabbi of Czarnigow gave me an introduction to the miracle-performing rabbi of Czarnobil, with whom I remained two weeks, and from whom I received introductions to six of his brothers, who were also miracle-performers. I visited them and many others, and was at length convinced that there was no truth in them. I was quite disgusted with them; my experience amongst them was such that volumes could be written upon the subject. However, I prefer to pray for them, and for those who believe in them, that the Lord with His light may reveal Himself to them, and use the great influence which these rabbis have upon the Jews for His kingdom, and change the strong faith which they have in the rabbi for belief in our blessed Lord and Saviour.

At this juncture I felt inclined to return home; but hearing of a rabbi named Hillel, who was approved by all parties of the Jews, I determined to see him first, and therefore went to Babrausk, the town where he resided.

CHAPTER X.

RABBI HILLEL; DESCRIPTION OF A "JESHIVAH,"—*i.e.*, RABBINICAL COLLEGE.

ON my arrival in Babrausk, I went to the residence of Rabbi Hillel, and was ushered by one of his attendants into his private room, where I saw a small thin figure dressed in *talleth* and *tephillin*,* sitting at the table with a folio book

---

* The talleth is a quadrangular garment with fringes, worn at morning prayers, as in Num. xv. 38, 39. The virtue of these fringes, in recalling the attention of their wearers to the Divine commands and preserving them from sins which they have been on the point of committing, is said to be very great; and the rabbinical writings contain some marvellous stories of things alleged to have happened before as well as since the giving of the law, related in confirmation of it. They are also considered as preservatives from the injuries of evil spirits.

The tephillin, or phylacteries, are of two sorts; one for the arm, the other for the head. The obligation to wear them is derived from Exod. xiii. 16, and Deut. vi. 6-9. They are made of the skin of some clean animal, in the form of a square box. The tephillin on the arm has but one compartment, that on the head has four, and has also impressed on one side of it the Hebrew letter, "*shin*"; and on the opposite side, a character resembling that letter, only having four points or heads, as the letter *shin* has three. This box is sewed to a thick skin, broader than the square of the box; of this skin is formed a loop, through which

of the Talmud. When I went up to him, he shook hands with me, saying: "*Shalom alechem,*"—*i.e.,* Peace unto you! I delivered the letter to him which I had brought from the Rabbi Pesach, who was his intimate friend and colleague. After reading it, he said, "Now, my dear son, what can I do for you?" I was so

passes a thong, with which the tephillin are fastened to the head. In the four compartments are enclosed four passages of the law, written on parchment and carefully folded. These parchments are commonly bound with some pure and well-washed hairs of a calf or cow, generally pulled from the tail; and the ends come out beyond the outer skin, to indicate that the schedules within are rightly made. But that skin is sewed and fastened together with very fine strings or cords, made from the sinews of a calf, cow, or bull; or if none of these are at hand, with soft and thin thongs or ligaments, cut out of a calf-skin. Through the loop of the box passes a long leather strap, which ought to be black on the outside, and on the inside any colour but red. With this strap the tephillin are bound to the head, so that the little box including the parchment rests on the forehead, below the hair, between the eyes, against the pericranium, that the Divine precepts may be fixed in the brain, which is supposed to contain the organs of thought, and to be the seat of the soul; that there may be more sanctity in prayer, and that the commandments of God may at the same time be confirmed and better observed. The strap is fastened on the back part of the head, with a knot tied in such a manner as is said to resemble the letter *daleth;* the ends of the straps pass over the shoulders, and hang down over each breast. The tephillin is similar to that of the head, but without the impressed characters and compartments; it is placed on the left arm just above the elbow, and fastened by a leather strap, with a noose, to the naked skin, on the inner part of the arm. The strap is twisted several times about the arm, and then three times round the middle finger; by some, three times round three of the fingers; and on the end of it is made the letter *jod.* These three Hebrew letters, "*shin, daleth,* and *jod,*" compose the Hebrew word "*Shaddai,*"—*i.e.,* Almighty.

deeply touched by the kind manner in which he spoke, that I resolved at once to be his disciple, and told him so, but he said in a calm, sweet voice, "My dear son, you are too young to study the Cabbalistic doctrine; you must first study more of the Talmud, and I would advise you to attend the *Jeshivah* first, and then, when you are duly qualified, I shall be glad to enrol you amongst my young men." He then gave me a note to the *Rosh Haishvah*, i.e., the principal of the college, who, after examining me, received me as a student in the highest class.

After being enrolled, I was presented by one of the college overseers to six wealthy Jews, with whom I should take my meals alternately on the six days of the week. Usually every student has seven hosts for the week, but as Rabbi Hillel wished me to spend the Sabbath with him, I needed only six other hosts. I very soon became a favourite amongst them, and each one wished to have me every day, but I preferred having a variety of hosts to being with only one. There were about a hundred and forty students in the college, and I had a very happy time there.

I now wrote to my mother, and upon receiving my letter she came to see me, and, if possible, to urge me to return home; she was, however, persuaded by Rabbi Hillel to leave me in the college, on condition that I should board with the principal of the college, to whom she offered a large sum of money. She then returned home, and I remained for two sessions in the college. My time during this year was occupied as follows: After attending morning service in the synagogue, I used to go, before my mother's visit, to my daily host; but after she left, I went to the principal's house, where I breakfasted, and then went to the college for the daily studies which occupied us until three o'clock in the afternoon. We then dined. At five o'clock we all assembled at the afternoon service, after which we had an hour of leisure, before the evening service. After this service we continued our studies until nine o'clock. This was the winter session plan; during the summer session, we had lectures after dinner until eight in the evening. The winter session commences after the Feast of Tabernacles, and ends two weeks before the Feast of the Passover; the summer session commences after Easter, and ends four weeks before the Jewish New Year.

That the reader may have a correct idea of the above named seasons, I will endeavour to give a description of the Jewish calendar, and at the same time to make him acquainted with the ceremonies of the Jewish feasts and fasts.

CHAPTER XI.

JEWISH CALENDAR, AND FEAST OF THE NEW YEAR; THE FAST OF GEDALIAH; THE DAYS OF PENITENCE; AND THE DAY OF ATONEMENT.

THE Jews reckon their dates from the creation of the world, according to which reckoning, in this Christian year, 1881, in the month of September, commenced the Jewish year of 5642. In a common year, there are twelve months, and 355 days. In leap year, thirteen months and 385 days. The names of the months are as follows: Tisri, Marchesvan, Chisleu, Teveth, Shevat, Adar, Veadar, Nisan, Ijar, Sivan, Tamuz, Ab, Elul,

The first feast of the year is *Rosh Hashanah, i.e.*, the beginning of the year, or the New Year, which included the first and second days of *Tisri*, which occurs sometimes in the beginning of September, or in the middle, or in the end of it, or sometimes even in the beginning of October. This feast is kept by cessation of all labour except what is necessary for the preparation of food, the repeating of long prayers in the synagogue, and going to a river to repeat prayers there also.

The New Year's feast is kept with great solemnity and dread, for the Jews believe that on this day God judges the world, and that three books are opened, in the first of which the names of the righteous, who observe the precepts of the Jewish Faith, are written; in the second, the names of the middling; in the third, the presumptuously wicked. The righteous are instantly written to everlasting life, and the wicked to the burning fire; but those, whose good and bad works are equal, remain in suspense until the Day of Atonement, which is on the 10th day of the same month. If they return from their evil works, are careful to repent, and reform their actions, then will their portion in life be with the righteous; but, if they do not repent, death is their destination. Therefore, when they come out of the synagogue on the first night of the festival, they salute each other thus: "To a good year shall ye be inscribed;" to which is answered, "Ye also." This feast is also called "The Feast of Trumpets," because in the morning service, after the lessons from the law and the prophets, they blow a trumpet or cornet, which is required to be made of ram's horn, in memory of the ram which was substituted for Isaac on Mount Moriah, which is believed to have happened on this day. The blowing of the cornet is preceded by the repetition, seven times, of the 47th Psalm, and a prayer, and when it has been sounded many times, the conductor of the service proclaims, "Happy is the people who know the joyful sound: they shall walk, O Lord! in the light of Thy countenance." Among many reasons assigned for the blowing of the cornet, one is to confound the accuser Satan that he may not be able to accuse the Jews before God.

A long service follows. The people return to their

homes, and at the beginning of their meal, they dip a piece of bread in honey, praying, "May it be the will of Thee, O my God, and the God of my fathers! that Thou shalt renew to us a good and sweet year." After dinner they go to the synagogue again, where they read the Psalms for a couple of hours. As soon as afternoon prayers are offered, they go to a river-side or to the sea, offer prayers, and then shake their garments over the water. This ceremony is considered by some to represent the casting away of their sins, and an accomplishment of the prophetical declaration in Micah vii. 19, "Thou wilt cast all their sins into the depths of the sea." Others think that a river should be chosen where there is fish, in order to put one in mind that we are taken away suddenly as fish caught in a net; therefore we ought to repent while we have the opportunity, and not put it off until to-morrow. The third day of Tisri is the Fast of Gedaliah, and is in remembrance of the murder of Gedaliah (Jer. xli. 2).

The first ten days of Tisri are called days of penitence, in which various confessions and supplications are added to the daily prayers. On the Sabbath before the Day of Atonement, which is called the Sabbath of Penitence, the rabbi delivers a discourse on the subject of repentance.

On the ninth day of this month, before daybreak, a peculiar ceremony takes place. All the members of the household are assembled, the males with cocks in their hands, the females with hens. The master of the house then stands up with his cock in his hands and reads a prayer (which all the family repeat after him) containing some verses of Psalm cvii. and ending with Job xxxiii. 23, 24. "If there be a messenger with him, an interpreter, one among a thousand, to show unto man his uprightness, then he is gracious unto him, and saith, 'Deliver him from going to the pit, I have found a ransom.'" Each one then swings the cock or hen, with his right hand, three times in a circle round his head, saying, "This is my commutation; this is my substitute; this is my atonement; let this cock or this hen be put to death for me, but let a fortunate life be vouchsafed to me and to all Israel." The fowls, which have all the time been bound by the legs, are then thrown on the ground, and are afterwards killed by the *shochet, i.e.*, he who holds the second office of rabbi, and whose duty it is to slay animals, it being unlawful to eat meat slain by any other man. The fowls used on this occasion are, if possible, to be white.

After the morning prayers they repair to the burial-ground, where they distribute the value of the expiating fowls in alms to the poor. The fowls are dressed in the afternoon and eaten before sunset. In the afternoon they go to the baths, and after purification they proceed to the synagogue to make their afternoon prayers, after which the men undergo the penance of voluntary flagellation, consisting of thirty-nine stripes (which, however, do not cause any pain at all), during which they make silent confession of their sins to God.

Before sunset they make a hearty meal, to prepare themselves for the approaching fast, which is of the most rigid kind, for after that meal, till the evening of the tenth day, they are forbidden to take any manner of sustenance, even so much as a drop of water. This fast lasts about twenty-eight hours.

After the meal the children go to their parents, who lay their hands upon them, and bless them. Then on the way to the synagogue, they endeavour to make reconciliation between themselves and any whom they have offended or injured during the past year. Then they enter the synagogue; which is splendidly illuminated with wax candles, which remain burning night and day till the fast is concluded. The opening service of this fast is a very solemn and imposing one. Nearly the whole congregation are dressed in white; the conductor stands at the desk, and the rulers on either side of him, with the rolls of the Pentateuch, adorned with silver crowns. After the opening prayer the rolls are again put into the ark, and the prayers are continued for more than three hours. Some, more devoted than others, remain all night in the synagogue. Those who return home, after the evening service, assemble again at daybreak, next morning, and continue in the synagogne all day, offering supplications and confessions; reading the lessons, and chanting psalms without intermission.

To give the reader an idea of the special confessions and supplications prescribed for the Day of Atonement, and which are repeated several times from the evening of the ninth day till the evening of the tenth; I quote the following:—

"Our God and the God of our ancestors! may our prayers come before Thee, and withdraw not Thyself from our supplications; for we are not so shameless of face, or hardened, as to declare in Thy presence, O Eternal, our God! and the God of our fathers, that we are righteous, and have not sinned; verily, we confess, we have sinned. We have trespassed, we have dealt treacherously, we have stolen, we have spoken slander, we have committed iniquity and have done wickedly, we have acted presumptuously, we have committed violence, we have framed falsehood, we have counselled evil, we have uttered lies, we have scorned, we have rebelled, we have blasphemed, we have revolted, we have acted perversely, we have transgressed, we have oppressed, we have been stiff-necked, we have acted wickedly, we have corrupted, we have done abominably, we have gone astray and have caused others to err, we have turned aside from Thy excellent precepts and institutions, and which hath not profited us; but Thou art just concerning all that is come upon us; for thou hast dealt most truly, but we have done wickedly. O may it then be acceptable in Thy presence, O Eternal, our God! and the God of our fathers, to pardon all our sins, and forgive all our iniquities, and grant us remission for all our transgressions. For the sin which we have committed against Thee, either by compulsion or voluntarily. And for the sin which we have committed against Thee, with a stubborn heart. For the sin which we have committed against Thee, out of ignorance. And for the sin which we have committed against Thee, with the utterance of our lips. For the sin which we have committed against Thee, with incestuous lewdness. And for the sin which we have committed against Thee, either publicly or secretly. For the sin which we have committed against Thee, with deliberate deceit. And for the sin which we have committed against Thee, with the speech of the mouth. For the sin which we have committed against Thee, by oppressing our neighbour. And for the sin which we have committed against Thee, by the evil cogitation of the heart. For the sin which we have committed against Thee, by assembling to commit fornication. And for the sin which we have committed against Thee, by acknowledging our sins with our mouth, but do not repent in our heart. For the sins which we have committed against Thee, by despising our parents and teachers. And for the sin which we have committed against Thee, either presumptuously or ignorantly. And for the sin which we have committed against Thee, with violence. And for the sin which we have committed against Thee, by the profanation of Thy name. For the sin which we have committed against Thee, with defiled lips. And for the sin which we have committed against Thee, with foolish expressions. For the sin which we have committed against Thee, with the evil imagination. And for the sin which we have committed against Thee, either knowingly or without deliberation.

"Yet, for all of them, O God of forgiveness! forgive us, pardon us, and grant us remission.

"For the sin which we have committed against Thee, by denying and lying. And for the sin which we have committed against Thee, by taking or giving a bribe. For the sin which we have committed against Thee, by scoffing. And for the sin which we have committed against Thee, by calumny. For the sin which we have committed against Thee, in traffic. And for the sin which we have committed against

Thee, in meat and drink. For the sin which we have committed against Thee, by extortion and usury. And for the sin which we have committed against Thee, by immodest discourse. For the sin which we have committed against Thee, by chattering. And for the sin which we have committed against Thee, with the twinkling of our eyes. For the sin which we have committed against Thee, with haughty looks. And for the sin which we have committed against Thee, with shamelessness.

"Yet for all of them, O God of forgiveness! forgive us, pardon us, and grant us remission.

"For the sin which we have committed against Thee, by shaking off the yoke of Thy law. And for the sin which we have committed against Thee, by litigiousness. For the sin which we have committed against Thee, by treachery to our neighbour. And for the sin which we have committed against Thee, by envy. For the sin which we have committed against Thee, by levity. And for the sin which we have committed against Thee, by our stubbornness. For the sin which we have committed against Thee, by running swiftly to do evil. And for the sin which we have committed against Thee, by tale-bearing. For the sin which we have committed against Thee, by false swearing. And for the sin which we have committed against Thee, by causeless enmity. For the sin which we have committed against Thee, by embezzlement. And for the sin which we have committed against Thee, by ecstasy.

"Yet for all of them, O God of forgiveness! forgive us, pardon us, and grant us remission.

"Also for the sins for which we were obliged to bring a burnt-offering. And for the sins for which we were obliged to bring a sin-offering. And for the sins for which we were obliged to bring an offering according to our ability. And for the sins for which we were obliged to bring a trespass-offering, for either a certain or a doubtful sin. And for the sins for which we were obliged to suffer the stripes of contumacy. And for the sins for which we were obliged to suffer flagellation. And for the sins for which we have incurred the penalty of extirpation, and being childless. And for the sins for which we have incurred the penalty of the four kinds of death formerly inflicted by our tribunal of justice—viz., stoning, burning, beheading, and strangling. For transgressing affirmative precepts or negative precepts, whether an action be appropriated thereto or not; as well those which are known to us, we have already made confession of them before Thee, O Lord our God, and the God of our fathers!"

Towards the evening, when the prayers of this Great Day of Atonement are concluded, they sound the cornet to announce that the fast is over. After that they offer the usual evening prayer, and when it is finished they depart from the synagogue, wishing each other a good year, and congratulating themselves on having performed the service of this solemnity with such precision and fervour, that even Satan himself is constrained to applaud their piety, and presuming that all their sins are forgiven. After blessing the new moon, they go to their homes rejoicing, and enjoy a good meal after their long fast.

CHAPTER XII.

THE FEAST OF TABERNACLES; HOSANNA RABBA, AND SIMCHATH TOURA.

THE fifteenth day of the month Tisri is the first day of the Feast of Tabernacles. This feast is mentioned in Leviticus xxiii. 39, 42, and is still strictly observed by the Jews. The pious Jews commence to build the booths directly when they come from the synagogue, in the evening of the tenth day. During the four days between the Day of Atonement and the Feast of Tabernacles, most Jews are employed in erecting and ornamenting their booths. Some erect them in their yards, some in their gardens, and others on the house-tops. The tabernacle or booth is a very slight erection, but must be at least eight feet high and ten feet square. The walls are of boards, and the top is of branches of trees. Inside, the walls are covered with carpeting, and hanging from the branches of the top are all kinds of fruit. During the festival week these tabernacles are accounted by the Jews as their proper dwellings; there they eat and drink, and many even sleep in them.

This feast commences on the evening of the fourteenth day. On returning from the synagogue, the whole family proceeds into the booth, and the master of the family takes a glass of wine in his right hand and says the *kedush*, *i.e.*, " the sanctification." After that he and the other members of the family who remain (women and children being exempt from abiding in the tabernacle) wash their hands, and, dipping some bread in honey, say the following blessing :— " Blessed art Thou, O Jehovah our God, King of the Universe ! who hath sanctified us with His commandments, and commanded us to dwell in a tabernacle." *

On the morning of the fifteenth they go to the synagogue, and, after a long service, they take a citron in the left hand and a branch of palm (myrtles and willows of the brook attached to it) in the right hand, and say the following grace : " Blessed art Thou, O Jehovah our God, King of the Universe ! who hath sanctified us with Thy commandments, and commanded us to take the palm branch. Blessed art Thou, O Lord our God, King of the Universe ! who hast let us live, and hath subsisted us, and let us arrive at the present season."

After this grace, which each says for himself, the whole congregation joins the conductor in singing the Psalms, from cxiii. to the end of cxviii. After the singing of the psalms, a roll of the law is taken out of the ark and carried to the pulpit, where it is usually read ; and then all whose hands are adorned with citrons, palm-branches, myrtles and willows of the

---

* This blessing they are obliged to say at every meal during the week of the feast. The following blessing is said only on the first night : " Blessed art Thou, O Jehovah our God, King of the Universe! who hast let us live, who hath subsisted us, and let us arrive at the present season."

brook, march in procession round the place where the man stands, who has the roll of the Pentateuch in his hands. This they do the next five days.

The seventh day of the feast is called *Hosanna Rabba*, i.e., assist with great succour. The eve of "Hosanna Rabba" is a night of dread, for it is believed by the Jews that in this night their doom is settled for good or evil. Therefore, they do not sleep the whole night, but are engaged, some in reading psalms, and some in reading other books which are holy to them. At daybreak they go to a bath to purify themselves and then repair to the synagogue, and after many prayers, and singing the Psalms from cxiii. to the end of cxviii., they take out all the rolls of the Law from the Ark and carry them to the pulpit, which is in the middle of the synagogue, and go round the pulpit seven times singing hymns, in which the word "hosanna," *i.e.*, "save, we beseech Thee," occurs often.

On the evening of "Hosanna Rabba" the feast of the eighth day commences, according to Numbers xxix. 35; and on the evening of the eighth day the feast of *Simchath Toura*—i.e., "Rejoicing of the Law." On this evening they go to the synagogue, where, after saying nearly the same prayers as on the night before, they take out all the rolls from the Ark, and during the seven processions round the pulpit, they who carry the rolls, and the whole congregation, sing ejaculatory prayers, which are particularly for this festival, as well as other songs. The rolls of the Pentateuch are again deposited in the Ark, and they all return home. Before partaking of supper they say the blessing of sanctification of the feast, and after supper they say the special grace for the feast.

In the morning of the ninth day, which is the last day of the feast, they go to the synagogue, and after repeating many prayers appointed for feast-days, they open the Ark, and, taking out the law, seven processions are performed as on the previous evening. When this is over, they take one of the rolls and read the portion for the day, which is from the first verse of the thirty-third chapter of Deuteronomy to the end, being the end of the law.

Immediately after this they take the second roll, and read another portion, which is from the beginning of Genesis to the end of the third verse of the second chapter. The reason of this is to show that man should always meditate upon the Word of God; and therefore as soon as they have finished the reading of the Pentateuch, they begin again, in order that they may be continually employed in reading and studying the Word of God.

Two members of the congregation, generally men of note, opulence, and known integrity, are chosen to stand up while these two portions are being read; one of them is nominated *Chasan Toura*—i.e., the "bridegroom of the law," and the second is called *Chasan Beroushith*—i.e., "the bridegroom of the beginning." The former stands when the end of the Pentateuch is being read, and the latter stands while the beginning is read. It is a day of great rejoicing to the Jews, that the Pentateuch, which is divided into weekly portions, has been read through, and that they have been spared another year to hear it again commenced.

After reading in a third roll, from Numbers xxix. 35, the same as the previous day, and the first chapter of the book of Joshua, a service in honour of the day is conducted, and the people then go to eat and drink in each other's houses; but no matter how great their entertainments, they never forget to offer their afternoon and evening prayers.

The Sabbath which follows the feast of "Simchath Toura" is called *Sabbath Beroushith*—*i.e.*, "the Sabbath in which the first portion of the Pentateuch is read." On this day the annual offices of the synagogue are ordered for the ensuing year.

In the second month, or according to Scripture, the eighth month, which is called Marchesvan, there are no feasts whatever.

CHAPTER XIII.

THE FEAST OF DEDICATION; THE FAST OF THE TENTH OF TEVETH; THE FAST OF ESTHER; AND THE FEAST OF PURIM.

THE commencement of the Feast of Dedication is on the twenty-fifth of Chisleu, which is the third, or according to the Scriptures, the ninth month of the year, and it continues eight days. This feast was instituted by Judas Maccabeus and his brethren, as a memorial of the purification of the temple, and the great victory which they obtained over Antiochus Epiphanus (about the year 168 B.C.), who had polluted the temple; therefore it was necessary to dedicate it again, and this dedication took place on the twenty-fifth day of this same month. The reason for keeping this feast eight days is, according to Jewish tradition, as follows: When the temple was cleansed and dedicated, and the priests came to light the lamps which were to burn continually before the Lord, according to Exod. xxvii. 20, 21, there was no more oil found (which was not polluted) than would be sufficient for one night, and it required eight days for the priests to prepare the oil, as it is commanded in Exod. xxvii. 20. But by a miracle performed by God, the small portion of oil continued to burn the eight days and nights until the priests obtained a fresh supply; therefore, to the present day the Jews light lamps at this feast in the synagogues and houses, in the following order:—

On the evening of the twenty-fourth of the month Chisleu, which is the first night of the feast *Chanoke* —*i.e.*, dedication—the household assembles. At the door is erected a lamp with eight branches; the master of the house takes a wax taper and lights one branch of the lamp, and repeats the following blessing: " Blessed art Thou, O Jehovah our God, King of the Universe! who hath sanctified us with Thy commandments, and commanded us to light the lamp of dedication. Blessed art Thou, O Jehovah our God, King of the Universe! who wrought miracles for our ancestors, in those days about this season. Blessed art Thou, O Jehovah our God, King of the Universe! that hath let us live, and hath subsisted us, and hath let us arrive at this season."

On the seven following nights the same ceremony is performed, with the addition of one light on each successive night. The prayers of this feast are the same as every day, but with the addition of Psalms cxiii. to cxviii. at the morning prayers, and the following in all the prayers for the day, even in the grace after meat : " For the miracles, and for the redemption, and for the mightiness, and for the salvation, and for the wars, which Thou didst perform for our fathers in those days, in this season. In the days of Matthias, son of Johanan, the High Priest, Ahashmonai and his sons, in the kingdom of Taban, the wicked did rise against Thy people Israel, to make them forget Thy law and to wander from the statutes of Thy will; and Thou, through Thy great compassion, didst arise unto them in the time of their trouble, Thou didst plead their cause, Thou didst judge their judgments, Thou didst revenge their vengeances, Thou didst deliver the strong into the hands of the weak, and the multitude into the hands of the few, and the impure into the hands of the undefiled, and the wicked into the hands of the righteous, and the haughty into the hands of the contemplators of Thy law; and unto Thyself Thou didst make a name, great and holy, in Thy world; and to Thy people Israel Thou didst perform a great deliverance and redemption on that day; and afterwards Thy children came into the avenue of Thy house and cleared Thy temple and cleansed Thy holy place, and did light up lights in the court of Thy holy house, and did fix those eight days of *Hanucah* to glorify and praise Thy great name."

The Feast of Dedication is kept strictly concerning the above described lighting of the lamps, and saying of the prayers; however, no servile work is forbidden during the eight days. This feast is merely kept as days of rejoicing for the wonders which God wrought for their forefathers. Friends, neighbours, and acquaintances meet together to enjoy the evenings of this week; children receive presents from their parents and friends; and the poor are also remembered.

On the tenth of Teveth is kept the fast which is mentioned in Zech. viii. 12, and is called the Fast of the Tenth. This fast is said to have been occasioned by the first approach of Nebuchadnezzar to the siege of Jerusalem, which, according to Jewish traditions, began this day.

Tanith Esther—*i.e.*, the fast of Esther—is kept on

the thirteenth of the month Adar. This fast is in commemoration of Esther's three days' and nights' fasting before she went to supplicate the King Ahasuerus on behalf of the Jews, who were marked out for destruction by Haman.

The feast of *Purim* takes place on the fourteenth of Adar; but it commences on the evening of the thirteenth, when, after the evening prayer and before they partake of food after the fast, a roll of parchment in which the book of Esther is written is spread out, in the manner of a letter, in reference to the words of Esther ix. 26, and the reader of the synagogue reads it from the beginning to the end; and as often as the reader mentions the name of Haman, the son of Hamedatha, the Agagite, the whole congregation stamp with their feet, and the children knock with little wooden hammers, as a memorial that they should endeavour to destroy the whole seed of Amalek. After the book of Esther has been read, they say prayers and thanksgivings for the deliverance of their nation, combined with curses on Haman and his wife, and blessings on Mordecai and Esther, which ends the evening service.

On the morning of the feast, the people go to the synagogue; and after the usual morning prayers, one of them takes a roll of the Pentateuch from the Ark, and reads in it Exod. xvii. 8 to the end of the chapter. When this has been read, and the roll returned to the Ark, the reader reads the book of Esther in the same manner as the evening before. To all the prayers, and to the grace after meat, on this day, the following prayer is added: "For the miracles, and for the redemption; and for the mightiness, and for the salvation; and for the wars which Thou didst perform for our fathers in those days, in this season; in the days of Mordecai and Esther, in Shushan, the capital city, when the wicked Haman rose against them; who endeavoured to extirpate, kill, and abolish all the Jews, from young to old, infants and women, in one day, on the thirteenth day of the twelfth month, called Oedar; and their substance to be for a spoil; and Thou, in Thy great compassion, didst destroy his counsel, and didst frustrate his designs; and Thou didst retort his work on his own head, and caused him and his sons to be hanged on a tree."

When the service in the synagogue is ended, they go home and spend the day in feasting and rejoicing, and sending presents to each other, and giving largely to the poor, for whom they keep open their houses as well as for the rich, that they all may come and enjoy; and it is delightful to see how rich and poor, young and old, enjoy themselves together without any question as to what class one or another belongs.

CHAPTER XIV.

THE MONTH NISAN; THE FEAST OF THE PASSOVER; THE FEAST OF PENTECOST; THE FAST OF THE SEVENTEENTH OF TAMUZ; AND THE STRICT FAST OF THE NINTH OF AB.

NISAN is the seventh month according to the modern Jewish reckoning, and the first according to Exod. xii. From the beginning of this month, preparations are made for the Feast of the Passover. The first thing is to bake the unleavened bread, which is made in thin round cakes about forty-five inches in circumference. These are used during the eight days of the Passover instead of the usual bread, and are made of flour and water only. All these preparations the richer classes make for themselves; they also provide for their poorer brethren, that they shall have a comfortable feast.

The Sabbath before the Passover is called *Sabbath Hagadoul*—i.e., the Great Sabbath. On that day the Rabbi expounds to the congregation the laws concerning the Passover, as in what manner the utensils are to be cleansed, and what may be used. The lecture lasts for about three hours without intermission, the congregation mostly standing.

On the evening of the thirteenth day of this month, the most careful and minute inquisition is made by the master of each family through every part of his house, in order to clear it of leavened bread and other articles of leaven, and in doing this he says the following blessing: "Blessed art Thou, O Jehovah, our God, King of the Universe! who hath sanctified us with His commandments, and commanded us to put away the leaven."

On the fourteenth day of the month before noon, the broken pieces of bread which the master of the house had collected in a vessel on the previous evening are solemnly burnt, together with the vessel. All the vessels which were used for leaven are put aside during the Passover, and in their place new ones are supplied; even the kitchen tables, shelves, and cupboards undergo a thorough purgation—first with hot water, then with cold.

On this day, the first-born son in every family fasts, in remembrance of God's great mercy in protecting the first-born of all the Jews on that memorable night in Egypt, when He smote all the first-born of the Egyptians.

In the evening of this day, the men assemble in the synagogue to usher in the festival with special prayers appointed for that evening's service; the women are occupied at home in decorating the tables and adorning the rooms with the most costly articles in honour of the festival. At the head of the table are placed three utensils of gold, silver, china, or common ware, according to circumstances; one of these is filled with salt water, in remembrance of the passage through the Red Sea; and the second with a kind of sweetmeat made from apples, nuts, sugar, &c., to the consistency of paste, in remembrance of the clay of which the children of Israel made bricks during their bondage in Egypt; in the third is a small lamb bone, about two inches long, which had been roasted in remembrance of the Passover; there are also bitter herbs on the table, in remembrance of their bitter bondage.

When the master of the house returns from the synagogue, the whole family from the lowest servant sits at the table. The reason why the servants are permitted at table on that night is to commemorate their being all servants and bondsmen in the land of Egypt. The master takes three cakes, and wrapping them carefully in a napkin, places them on a large silver or china plate, and covers them with another napkin. He then takes a plate on which has been placed a small lamb bone, an egg, some lettuce, chervil, parsley and celery, and puts it on the cakes; a glass of wine is filled for each person; the master then takes his glass in his hand, and pronounces the following blessing: "Blessed art Thou, O Jehovah our God, King of the Universe! the Creator of the fruit of the vine; blessed art Thou, O Jehovah our God, King of the Universe! who hath chosen us above any nation, and exalted us above any language, and sanctified us with His commandments; and hath vouchsafed unto us, O Jehovah our God, thy love. This is the time of the feast of unleavened bread—the time of our redemption with love and holy convocation; a memorial of the departure from Egypt. For us thou hast chosen, and us Thou hast sanctified of all the nations, and hast sanctified this season with love and favour, with joy and gladness, and hast made us to inherit. Blessed art Thou, O Jehovah, the Sanctifier! And blessed art Thou, O Jehovah our God, King of the Universe! that hath let us live, and hath subsisted us, and hath let us arrive at this season." Then, leaning in a stately manner on his left arm upon a couch, as an indication of the liberty which the Israelites regained when they departed from Egypt, the master drinks his glass of wine, in which he is followed by the whole company. Having emptied their glasses, they wash their hands, and dip some of the bitter herbs in the salt water, and eat them while the master pronounces another benediction. He then unfolds the napkins which contain the three cakes, and taking the middle cake, breaks it in two, replaces one of the pieces between the two whole cakes, and conceals the other folded in a napkin under the cushion on which he leans.* After removing the plate which was placed upon the cakes, he and the whole company together lift up the plate with the cakes, and say as follows: "This is the bread of poverty and affliction, which our fathers did eat in Egypt. Whosoever hungers, let him come and eat. Whosoever needs, let him come and eat of the paschal lamb. This year we are here, the next, God willing, we shall be in the land of Israel (*i.e.*, Palestine). This year we are servants, the next, if God will, we shall be free." The plate is again placed on the cakes, and another glass of wine is filled for each. They then make the children inquire into the meaning of the festival. If none are present, then some adult proposes

* See explanation in chap. xvi. part ii.

the prescribed form of questions, which are answered by all who are able to read, who give an account of the captivity and slavery of the Jewish nation in Egypt; their deliverance by Moses, who instituted and first celebrated this feast on the night preceding the departure of the Israelites from Egypt. This recital is followed by some psalms and hymns, which the master chants in a loud voice, followed by all who can read. They then drink the second glass of wine, after which they again wash their hands. The master then takes one of the cakes from between the napkins, and after saying the blessing, he breaks it, and gives a piece to each one round the table. He then takes the third cake, and breaks it into pieces about the size of an olive, and puts some bitter herbs between the pieces, in remembrance that their forefathers, when in Egypt, had their lives embittered by their task-masters. Between the pieces of cake he also puts some of the pastry, which has the appearance of clay, in remembrance of the time when their forefathers were working in clay, making bricks under their cruel task-masters. He then hands a portion to each round the table, and says with a loud voice, joined by all the company, the following words: "So has done Hillel" (one of the greatest rabbis) "in the time when the sanctuary existed. He did wrap up unleavened bread with bitter herbs, and did eat them together, to fulfil what is said (in the twelfth chapter of Exodus and the eighth verse): "Unleavened bread, and with bitter herbs they shall eat it." After partaking of supper, the master takes the piece of cake which he had under the cushion, and distributes a piece of it to each of the company, which all eat with great solemnity.* The third glass of wine is then filled for each of the household, and after the usual grace after meat is said, they drink it, and immediately fill it again for the fourth and last time, as the Jews on this night must drink neither less nor more than four glasses of wine. A larger glass than all is now filled for Elijah, the prophet, who is believed to make his appearance in every Jewish house on this night. The door is now opened by some of the household, and the whole company rise from their seats, saying, *Baruch Haba*—i.e., "Blessed is he that cometh;" and, after a short prayer, the door is closed again, and the company retake their seats, and sing some psalms and hymns, specially appointed for the occasion, which occupies them until almost midnight. They then drink their last glass of wine, and retire to rest. The same ceremony is repeated on the second night of the Passover.

The Passover is kept seven days in Palestine and eight days in other lands, during which time no leavened bread may be eaten. In Palestine, the first and last days; in other countries, the first two and the last two are kept as days of high solemnity, being celebrated with great pomp, extraordinary services in the synagogue, and by ceasing from all labour. The four intermediate days, or in Palestine the five, are kept as half holidays.

The Feast of Pentecost, which derives its name from the Greek, signifies the fifth day after the feast of unleavened bread. Moses called it the feast of weeks, and it is also called the feast of the first fruits, because

* See explanation in chap. xvi. part ii.

it occurred about the beginning of the harvest; therefore it was instituted as a thanksgiving to God for the fruits of the earth. The Jews celebrate it now, only in commemoration of the giving of the Law, which took place on the fiftieth day after the departure from Egypt. This feast includes two days, which are kept with the same strictness as the first two days of the Passover, and is celebrated with peculiar services in the synagogue, three times a day. In some countries the synagogues and the houses are decorated with flowers and odoriferous herbs. The book of Ruth is read in the synagogue, because what is narrated there took place at the time of harvest.

On the eve of the first day of the feast they occupy themselves in reading portions from the Bible and from the Talmud, and they continue doing so during the whole night.

The seventeenth of Tamuz is a solemn fast, which is called by Zechariah, chap. viii. ver. 19, "the fast of the fourth month." It is now kept on account of several mournful events. First, the breaking of the Tables of the Law, by Moses; second, the ceasing of the daily sacrifice in the first temple; third, the entrance of the Romans into Jerusalem, through a breach in the walls, after the siege by Titus; all of which unhappy events occurred on this day.

The fast of the ninth of Ab is as strict as the fast of the Day of Atonement, and is called in Zech. viii. 19, "the fast of the fifth month." It is kept on account of the burning of the sanctuary at Jerusalem by Nebuchadnezzar, the king of Babylon, and also on account of the destruction of the second temple by Titus, which occurred on the same day. All labour is suspended, and every Jew who is in health abstains from all meat and drink from before sunset on the eighth day of Ab, when the fast commences, until after sunset on the ninth, when it ends.

On the eighth of Ab, before sunset, after partaking of their usual meal, the men sit on the floor at a low table, on which some bread, ashes, and eggs are placed, of which they partake a little. They then proceed to the synagogue, and take off their shoes; the evening prayer is then offered, after which they sit upon the floor, while the reader of the synagogue, also seated on the floor, reads the book of the Lamentations of Jeremiah. Very early, on the morning of the ninth day, and after the usual prayers (but without putting on their talleth and tephillin, see chap. x.), they take a roll of the Pentateuch from the Ark, and read in it a portion from Deut. xxiv. 25 to end of 40, and from Jer. viii. 13 to ix. 24. They then replace the roll, and the whole congregation, seated on the floor, chant mournful hymns until noon. When the service is over, they visit the cemetery and then return home. Before sunset they go again to the synagogue, and offer the afternoon prayers in talleth and tephillin. A portion from the Pentateuch is read, in Exod. xxxi. 11-14 and xxxiv. 1-10; also from the Prophecy of Isa. lv. 6 to the end of lvi. 7. When the stars appear, they make their evening prayers and return home to break the fast of the last twenty-eight hours.

The sixth month according to the Scriptures, or the last month according to the present reckoning of the

Jews, is called Elul; it is considered as a month of repentance, and in order to remind the Jews of it, they blow a horn in the synagogue every day, in this month, after the morning prayers. During the last week they rise two or three hours before daybreak, and go to the synagogue to make prayers and supplications, which last till daybreak.

CHAPTER XV.

CELEBRATION OF THE JEWISH SABBATH.

THE Jewish Sabbath commences at sunset on Friday, and terminates at sunset on Saturday. The Jews, however, lengthen it by discontinuing business an hour or two before sunset on Friday, and not resuming it until an hour or two after sunset on Saturday. Nearly all the Jews take a bath on the Friday, and the more pious do so directly after the noon hour. Having washed, they trim their hair and pare their nails, beginning with the left hand, as follows: First, the third; next, the forefinger; then the little one, then the middle finger, and lastly, the thumb. On the right hand, first the forefinger, next the third, then the thumb, then the middle finger, and lastly, the little one. This order is maintained because they superstitiously deem it improper to cut the nails on two adjoining fingers. What is done with the parings may be a matter of indifference to the Gentiles, but not so to the Jews, who are taught in the Talmud (Book, Moed Katon, folio 18, column 1), that " he that throws them on the ground is ungodly; he that buries them is just; he that burns them is a pious and perfect one." When they return from the bath they find the table spread with a clean cloth, upon which are laid two loaves, which were baked on the Friday morning specially for the Sabbath; also, silver candlesticks or copper ones, according to circumstances. The loaves are covered with a clean napkin; they are to remind the Jews of the manna in the wilderness, of which a double quantity fell on the sixth day, but none on the Sabbath.

Every article of food which is necessary for the Sabbath is prepared and dressed on the Friday before sunset, and many of the pious Jews, even those who have numerous servants, do something with their own hand in honour of the Sabbath. The Talmud, in the Book Sabbat, folio 119, gives examples of great rabbis doing so. For instance, "Rabbi Chasdam chopped the herbs, the very learned Rabbam and Rabbi Joseph clave the wood, Rabbi Siram lit the fire, Rabbi Nachman swept the house and prepared the table."

A little before sunset the whole family are dressed in Sabbath attire, and a great number of candles are lighted by the women of the household. Every woman must light at least one candle to atone for the crime of their mother Eve, who, by eating of the forbidden fruit, first extinguished the light of the world. Immediately the candle is lit the woman stretches both her hands towards it, and says: "Blessed art Thou, O Jehovah our God, King of the Universe! who hast sanctified us with Thy precepts, and commanded us to light the Sabbath lamps." (On feast days they say "to light the light of the feast.") The men are also attired in their best clothes, and they hasten a little before sunset to the synagogue to receive the Sabbath, which they compare to a royal bride. After chanting the 107th Psalm, and a portion from the book of Sohar (one of the cabalistic books), they make their afternoon prayers, and commence the service of receiving the Sabbath, which begins with the 95th Psalm to the end of the 99th, after which a short prayer is repeated in a low voice, and then the following hymn is chanted:—

"Come, my beloved, to meet the bride; the presence of the Sabbath let us receive. Come, my beloved, &c.

"Keep and remember it; both words did the one peculiar God cause us to hear, with one expression: the Eternal is a Unity, and His name is Unity: to Him appertaineth renown, glory, and praise. Come, my beloved," &c.

"Come, let us go to meet the Sabbath; for it is the fountain of blessing: in the beginning, of old was it appointed; for though last in creation, yet it was first in the design of God. Come, my beloved," &c.

"O thou sanctuary of the king, O royal city! arise and come forth from thy subversion; thou hast dwelt long enough in the abode of calamity, for He will now pity thee with kindness. Come, my beloved," &c.

"Shake off the dust, arise, O my people! and adorn thyself with thy beautiful attire; for by the hand of Jesse the Bethlehemite, redemption draweth nigh to my soul. Come, my beloved," &c.

"Rouse thyself, rouse thyself; arise, shine, for thy light is come. Awake, awake, utter a song; for the glory of the Lord is revealed upon thee. Come, my beloved," &c.

"O be not ashamed, neither be thou confounded. Why art thou cast down? Why art thou disquieted?

In thee the poor of my people shall take refuge, and the city shall be built on her own heap. Come, my beloved," &c.

"They who spoil thee, shall become a spoil; and they that swallow thee up, shall be removed far away: thy God will rejoice in thee, as the bridegroom rejoiceth in his bride. Come, my beloved," &c.

"On the right hand, and on the left, shalt thou be extended; and the Lord shalt thou fear: through the means of a man, the descendant of Pharez, will we rejoice and be glad. Come, my beloved," &c.

"O come in peace, thou crown of thy husband; also with joy and mirth in the midst of the faithful, of the beloved people. Enter, O bride! Enter, O bride! Come, my beloved," &c.

After repeating many prayers from the Jewish prayer-book, they return home and bless their children, saying to each of their sons: "God make thee as Ephraim and Manasseh;" and to each daughter, "God make thee as Sarah and Rebekah, Rachel and Leah."

Immediately after that, the whole family seat themselves at the table, and the master of the house takes a glass of wine, or any other liquor, and says the *Kedoush*, *i.e.*, sanctification of the Sabbath; it consists of the first three verses of the second chapter of Genesis, and the following grace: "Blessed art Thou, O Jehovah, our God, King of the Universe! the Creator of the fruit of the vine. Blessed art Thou, O Lord our God, King of the Universe! who hast sanctified us with Thy commandments, and delightest in us; and with love and favour hast made us to inherit the holy Sabbath, for a memorial of the work of the creation; for that day was the first of those called holy; a remembrance of the going forth from Egypt; for Thou hast chosen us, and sanctified us above all people; and with love and favour hast Thou made us to inherit Thy holy Sabbath. Blessed art Thou, O Jehovah, who sanctifiest the Sabbath." He then drinks some of the wine, and presents the glass to the rest of the family, who also drink of it. Supper follows immediately, and between the courses hymns are sung, and the meal ends with a long grace, including these words: " Be graciously pleased, O Lord our God! to fortify us in Thy commandments, and in the commandment of the seventh day, this great and holy Sabbath; for this day is great and holy before Thee for repose, and to have rest thereon with love, according as it was Thy pleasure to command: and with Thy favour, O Lord our God! grant us rest thereon, that there be no trouble, sorrow, or sighing on this day of our repose: and grant us, O Lord our God! to behold the consolation of Zion, Thy city, and the building of Jerusalem, Thy holy city, for Thou art the Lord of salvation and the Lord of consolations.

"O the merciful! He shall let us inherit the day which is all Sabbath and the life of eternal rest.

"O the merciful! He shall make us worthy to behold the days of the Messiah, and that we may enjoy life in futurity."

In the morning they go to the synagogue, and after a long service, the roll of the Pentateuch is taken from the Ark and carried with great ceremony to the desk, where the weekly portion is read. At the conclusion of the reading one Jew elevates the roll in such a manner that the writing may be seen by the congregation, who shout: "And this is the law which Moses set before the children of Israel," &c. They then read a portion from the Prophets, and offer prayers for the rulers of the country, for the congregation, and for all the Israelites, wherever they may be. The roll is then returned with great ceremony to the Ark, and after another long service they return to their homes. At dinner, similar ceremonies are observed to those of supper on the previous evening.

About three o'clock in the afternoon, the rabbi, or some other preacher, delivers a sermon in the synagogue, which occupies two or three hours, and then they perform the afternoon service. After that, in the summer time, they read a chapter from the Talmud, in the book called, "The Advice of the Fathers;" in the winter they read Ps. civ., and from cxx. to the end of cxxxiv. They return home again and partake of the last Sabbath meal, called "*Shaloush Soodous*," *i.e.*, "the third meal;" for the Jews take three meals specially appointed for the Sabbath—the first on Friday evening, the second on Saturday at noon, and the third a little before sunset.

Every Jew is glad to have a guest at his Sabbath meals, and in this way the poor who have no families (for those who have families are provided with every Sabbath necessary by the Jewish community) are entertained at the houses of the independent,—even the poorest sitting at the table of the wealthiest; those who are able receive several such guests, and when the Sabbath is over, they present them with money. In the evening they go again to the synagogue to offer the evening prayers; they extend this service to a later hour than usual, for the following reasons: first, to lengthen the Sabbath; and second, to extend the respite enjoyed on the Sabbath by the wicked in hell, whose punishment is, according to Jewish tradition, suspended immediately on the chanting of the hymn for receiving the Sabbath, on Friday evening, until the evening prayers on Saturday are finished.

On their return from the synagogue the ceremony of הכדלה, *Habdala, i.e.,* "division or separation" (because this ceremony divides the Sabbath from the other days of the week), takes place. It is performed as follows: A wax candle, composed of several tapers twisted together like a cable, and lighted, is placed in the hand of a child, who holds it while the master of the family, taking a silver goblet, or a glass, of wine in his right hand, and a silver box of spices in his left, says the following blessing: "Behold, God is my salvation; I will trust and not be afraid; for the Lord Jehovah is my strength and song; He also is become my salvation. Therefore, with joy shall ye draw water out of the wells of salvation. Salvation belongeth unto the Lord: Thy blessing is upon Thy people. Selah. The Lord of Hosts is with us; the God of Jacob is our refuge. Selah. The Jews had light, and gladness, and joy, and honour.—Thus may it also be unto us.—I will take the cup of salvation, and call upon the name of the Lord. Blessed art Thou, O Lord our God, King of the Universe! who hast created the fruit of the vine." Then taking the glass of wine in his left hand, and the box of spices in his right, he says: "Blessed art Thou, O Jehovah our God, King of the Universe! who hast created diverse spices." Here he smells the spices and presents them to the family, that they may have the same gratification. Then standing near the candle or lamp, he looks at it with great attention, and also at his finger-nails, and says: "Blessed art Thou, O Lord our God, King of the Universe! who hast created the light of the fire." Then taking the wine again in his right hand, he says: "Blessed art Thou, O Lord our God, King of the Universe! who hast made a distinction between things sacred and profane; between light and darkness; between Israel and other nations; between the seventh day and the six days of labour. Blessed art Thou, O Jehovah our God! who hast made a distinction between things sacred and profane."

This ceremony is also performed in the synagogue for the benefit of the poor, who cannot bear the expense of performing it at home, or for those who have no males in their houses to conduct it for them. The Sabbath ends with this ceremony, and all are at liberty to resume their usual weekly employments.

CHAPTER XVI.

MY FURTHER CONNECTION WITH RABBI HILLEL; TWO JOURNEYS TO THE GRAND RABBI OF THE JEWISH SECT CALLED CHABAD; AND A DESCRIPTION OF THE SECT.

IN chapter x. I related somewhat of my connection with Rabbi Hillel. I now wish to enlarge upon it, in order to introduce much of great interest in the Russian Jewish life, and more particularly of the Jewish sect called Chabad. I have told you how my time was spent in the *Jeshivah* during the five days, from Sunday to Thursday. You shall now hear how I passed the Friday and Saturday in Rabbi Hillel's house.

After morning prayers and breakfast, I chanted the weekly portion from the Pentateuch, once in Hebrew and twice in the Aramaic language, as also a portion from the Prophets. Then I went to Rabbi Hillel's house, where I remained till Sunday morning, and was engaged as follows: In the first place, Rabbi Hillel took me and his grandson, Phinehas, who was a little older than myself, to the baths, where, after being washed with warm water, we all three went into the basin; and the Rabbi taught us two what angels we should bear in mind during the purification by immersion, and how many times we needed to immerse ourselves in order to be holy for the receiving of the special soul, which the Jews believe is to be received for the Sabbath.

On returning from the baths, and after being dressed in our best attire, we chanted the Song of Solomon, and then we read the weekly portion in the cabalistic book, Sohar, which Rabbi Hillel explained to us. I then accompanied Phinehas to an adjoining hall, used as a synagogue, where many Jews were assembled for prayer. At the conclusion of these afternoon prayers, Rabbi Hillel came from his study and delivered a sermon, which lasted for about half an hour. Then commenced the service of receiving the Sabbath, and when finished, I accompanied Phinehas to the rabbi's study; he received us and blessed us with great solemnity. We then proceeded to the dining hall, where, at a long table, were seated about twenty rabbinical candidates, who rose in respect to the rabbi when we entered. While we partook of supper, hymns were sung, and a great number of Jews assembled to hear the rabbi, who addressed them after every Sabbath meal for about an hour before leaving the table, setting forth cabalistic doctrine.

Rabbi Hillel belonged to the Jewish sect called Chabad, whose rabbis are all cabalists, and whose doctrine is understood only by the learned of this sect.

On Saturday morning we again went to the basin for purification by immersion, as we were accustomed to do every day before prayer. After the morning service, dinner and the preaching were conducted in the same manner as on the previous evening. After dinner Phinehas and I studied the book Medrash, *i.e.*, "a commentary on the Bible. Rabbi Hillel's address, after the third Sabbath meal, was much longer than that after the other meals; and after *Habdala* (see chap. xv.) I went with Phinehas to the rabbi's study, where he gave us a lesson in cabalistic lore, which lasted for more than two hours. I am not able to express to my readers the delight I had in those lessons, for they were all about the angels and all kinds of spiritual things; and when I went to bed, I dreamed that I was walking about in heaven, seeing the angels, and calling them by their names.

During the two sessions that I was in Babrausk, I made two journeys with Rabbi Hillel to Lubavitz, the town where the grand rabbi had his residence.

The sect Chabad is not older than the end of the eighteenth century, and was established by Rabbi Zalmen Schnerson, a very great and learned man in Talmudistic and cabalistic lore. He was a disciple of the cabalistic Grand Rabbi Ber of Mezritz. Until the death of Rabbi Ber, the cabalistic doctrine was confined only to the chosen rabbis; but Rabbi Zalmen Schnerson was of the opinion that it ought to be preached and taught to every one. He therefore founded a sect called חב״ד, *Chabad*. These three Hebrew letters are the initials of three Hebrew words which signify *Wisdom, Understanding, Knowledge*. He resided in a small town in the government Mohilew, where this doctrine was very soon acknowledged. A large number of disciples were rapidly joined to him and soon became a sect, which from its commencement was persecuted by the Jews, who accused Rabbi Schnerson before the Russian Government of proclaiming himself king of the Jews, and of preparing to return to Palestine with a large number of Jewish followers whose names were in his register; also, of sending money to the Turkish Government for the purpose of obtaining its assistance in this undertaking. He was arrested by the command of the Emperor Paul and escorted to St. Petersburg, where, after a lengthened imprisonment, his case was tried, and the names on his register were found to be those of his sect, who have nothing to do with political affairs; the sending money to Turkey was for the relief of the poor of the sect dwelling in Palestine. The rabbi was therefore acquitted, and the sect continued to increase. He was soon after again accused by the Jews and imprisoned by the Emperor Paul, and would have been sent to Siberia, had not the death of the emperor, and the succession of Alexander I., given an opportunity for his release. It is said by the Jews that he soon became a favourite with Alexander I. on account of his great ability, and that he advised the emperor in many things relative to the Russian-French war in 1812.

Rabbi Schnerson died in 1813 on the way when he fled from the French army, who overran the province in that year. He was buried in Gadiatz, in the province of Poltava. A synagogue has been built over his grave, and to this day his followers make pilgrimages to the spot, where they offer long prayers, and place their requests, written on paper, in the tomb, in the hope that the rabbi hears and reads them. After the death of their leader, the sect, which was very numerous, divided into two parts, one of which chose as leader Rabbi Aaron, a disciple of the late rabbi; the other division chose Rabbi Ber, the eldest son of Rabbi Salmen Schnerson. His second son, Rabbi Moses, who was in every way more intellectual and learned than the elder son, was offended, and went away to St. Petersburg, where he joined the Greek Church, was baptised into the same, and appointed to a high office amongst its leaders.

Rabbi Aaron died without a successor, when the two divisions reunited under the leadership of Rabbi Mendul (son-in-law of Rabbi Ber Schnerson), who, for his great learning, was much honoured, not only by his own sect but also by the Jews in general. He was the grand rabbi of the sect, and to him I made the two journeys in company with Rabbi Hillel, as already mentioned.

The first of these journeys was made before the Feast of Dedication, and we remained with the rabbi until after the feast. We were accompanied also by Phinehas, and by more than twenty candidates for the office of rabbi. Our journey was a very lively one, and in every town or village through which we passed we were met by the Jews with great demonstrations and respect.

In Lubavitz, Rabbi Hillel introduced me to the Grand Rabbi Mendul Schnerson, who laid his hand upon me and blessed me. Phinehas also introduced me to all the sons of the grand rabbi. The small town was full of strangers, so that nearly every house became an inn. The grand rabbi preached once a week, and his sermon was repeated every day of the week by his sons and by the professional repeaters.

The strangers run from one repeater to another until they know the sermon by heart.

Our second journey was before the feast of weeks, or Pentecost. During this visit I saw about 500 rabbis, who came to visit the grand rabbi. The rabbis of this sect visit their grand rabbi every year at Pentecost, when they hold council under his superintendence for the arrangement of the affairs of the sect. The Chabad is the most zealous of all the Jewish sects. Its adherents are occupied much more with spiritual than with worldly things. Among themselves they are as brethren, the poorest mingling with the rich, going without ceremony to them in any need, and obtaining immediate relief. A poor teacher was accustomed to come to me in his necessity, and I remember how, one morning, when he came very early, before I was up, and told me he needed money, I just bid him take my keys, and help himself to as much as he required, knowing that he would not take any undue advantage of this liberty. Many of this sect mortify their bodies, and some go to great extremes. For instance, in my eighteenth year I used to go in the morning, fasting, to the synagogue, remaining there until one o'clock without food, and engaged the whole time in prayer and in reading books which are holy to the Jews. And when I did go home, where the table was spread with the best food, I would take a great deal of salt with it, in order to destroy the good taste; and, while still hungry, I often pushed away the food, saying, "Satan, do not make me eat like Esau." I frequently left my comfortable bed, and lay upon the bare floor. Twice a week, I sat up the whole night, reading in the Talmud and other holy books, all the time imagining myself surrounded by angels.

My prayers, which lasted for about three hours, I accompanied with snapping of my fingers and other gesticulations, thinking myself transformed and walking spiritually in heaven. So enrapt was I in these thoughts that I knew nothing of what was going on around me. I usually sung or chanted my prayers. The following is a specimen of one song of my own composition, which I used more frequently than others:—

SONG OF MOSES.

Sing unto the Lord—Israel's mighty Lord!
   For o'er Pharaoh's host—
    O'er proud Egypt's boast,
Dark sea waves He poured.

SONG OF MOSES.

Strength, and song, and sure salvation,
  Is Jehovah unto me;
I will rear an habitation
  Unto the God that smote the sea.

Lord, Thou art my God—and my father's God;
    I will sing Thy praise
    In triumphant lays,
  Whose arm swayed the flood.
Waters great the foe did cover;
  Down they sank, as still as a stone;
While the people, Lord, passed over,
  Which Thou hadst purchased for Thine own.

Who is like to Thee?—like, O Lord, to Thee?
    Thou, with out-stretched hand,
    Broughtst Thy chosen band
  Dry-shod through the sea!
Dark was Egypt's night of sorrow;
  Thick their dead lay on the shore,
Brightly breaks Thine Israel's morrow,
  For they shall see the foe no more.

Praises to Thy name!—to Thy holy name!
    At Thy nostrils' breath
    Sank Thy foes in death;
  Great fear on them came.
Palestina—Moab—Edom,
  Faint with dread shall melt away;
For the hand that wrought our freedom,
  He, in His wrath, on them shall lay.

Sing with timbrel's sound—timbrel's festive sound,
    Sing with joyful voice!
    Let each heart rejoice!
  And with gladness bound.
Praised be Thou to Everlasting!
  Thou hast triumphed gloriously!
Man of War!—Jehovah!—casting
  Horse and rider in the sea.

Adapted to the Hebrew Melody by Mrs. COUSIN (*Melrose*).

CHAPTER XVII.

HOW I TRIED TO ESTABLISH A NEW JEWISH SECT; MY STUDIES IN THE GRAND RABBINICAL ACADEMY OF VALOZIN; THE JEWISH THEOLOGY IN GENERAL, AND THE CHABAD IN PARTICULAR.

A YEAR'S study in the *Jeshivah*, my connection with Rabbi Hillel, and the influence of the sect Chabad, all tended to make my naturally strong will still stronger in the determination to carry out every undertaking. I was over fourteen when I resolved to establish a new Jewish sect of which I should be the grand rabbi; which resolution I also commenced to carry out as soon as I returned home from Babrausk. I succeeded in getting sixteen disciples, young men of my own age, but was soon disturbed by their parents; I therefore decided to postpone this undertaking to a more suitable period, when I should really be a rabbi. In order to prepare myself properly for that office, I went, with my mother's consent, to the Grand Rabbinical Academy of Valozin, in the government of Minsk, where I studied for two years, and then went to the Grand Rabbi Mendul of Lubawitz, leader of the Chabad, and studied under him for one year.

Among the large number of books which I studied during these three years was the Jewish

Theology of which I will give a specimen in this chapter.

Concerning God.

The doctrine concerning God is, according to modern Jews in general, identical with that of the pantheists, who believe God to be revealed everywhere and in everything, from the stars to the blades of grass. The Chabad sect, though they profess, like other Jews, to be monotheists, do in reality approach the doctrine of the Trinity, for they believe as follows: God is אור אין סוף, "*Oer Ain Soph*" (this term is frequently used by the cabalists), *i.e.*, "*Infinite Light;*" and as He has no end, so He has also no beginning. This is the origin of the Godhead. This *Oer Ain Soph* is divided by the sect Chabad into three spiritual heads or beginnings. The first is a head which has no beginning, and is compared to the human mind, before it conceives any idea; the second is called a beginning which is imperceptible, and is compared to the human thoughts; the third is called a perceptible beginning, and is compared to the expression of the human thoughts in words. These three heads or beginnings, like the human mind, thoughts, and words, are undivided. The last named head or beginning, which is the *word* of the *Oer Ain Soph*, is the spiritual source of all things, as it is written in Psalm xxxiii. ver. 6, "By the word of Jehovah were the heavens made, and all the host of them by the breath of His mouth." Before the world was created, all space was filled with the light which is called *Oer Ain Soph;* but when the Divine mind conceived the creation of the universe, the supreme light confined itself, leaving a space all around it which still contained some vestiges of the Infinite Light; the latter is called *Momaloe Kal Almin, i.e.* "filling the universe," and the former, *Soevoev Kal, Almin, i.e.,* "surrounding the universe." These two infinities are united through ten splendours or channels which are denominated, Supreme, Crown, Wisdom, Understanding, Mercy, Power, Beauty, Victory, Glory, Stability, and Sovereignty.

These are not like instruments used by an agent, distinct and separate from the hand which employs them, but essential instruments of Divine communication, substantially existing in the Divine nature, and proceeding from it through the medium of the first offspring of Deity, as rays issuing from the sun are instruments of heat, of the same nature as their source. Through these channels of light, all things have proceeded from the first emanation of Deity; things celestial, spiritual, angelic, and material. These constitute four worlds: *Aziluth*, or the world of emanation, proceeding from the primordial light, through the medium of the first-born of Infinity, and comprehending all the excellencies of the inferior worlds without any of their imperfections; *Bria*, or the world of creation, containing those spiritual beings which derive their existence immediately from the Aziluthic world; *Jetsira*, or the formative world, containing those spiritual substances which derive their immediate origin from the Briatic world; *Ashia*, or the material world, including all those substances which are capable of composition, motion, division, generation, and corruption; this world consists of the very dregs of emanation and is the residence of evil spirits.

Concerning Angels.

Of the Jewish traditions concerning angels, and the time of their creation, there are different accounts given by different rabbis. One says the angels were created on the second day; another says they were created on the fifth; other rabbis say that there are some angels which continue for ever, being those which were created on the second day; but those who were created on the fifth day are perishable. Another rabbi contradicts them all by saying that before the creation of the world God created the shape of the holy angels, who were the beginning of all created beings, and were derived from the glance of His glory. One rabbi affirms that four classes of ministering angels sing praises in the presence of the holy and blessed God. The first class, at the head of which is Michael, is on His right hand; the second, under Gabriel, on His left; the third, under Uriel, before Him; the fourth, under Raphael, behind Him; and the Divine Majesty is in the midst, seated on a throne, high and lifted up. Some angels are said to be created from fire; others from water; others from wind; and, according to some rabbis, there is an angel created by every word that proceeds out of the mouth of God. The hierarchy of the angels is said by some rabbis to include ten orders, to which they have assigned the following appellations: Chaioth-Hakkodesh, Seraphim, Ophanim,

Erellim, Chasmalim, Melachim, Elohim, Beni-Elohim, Cherubim, and Ishim.

The rabbis ascribe to one angel, who is called Metatron, more illustrious prerogatives than to any other of the heavenly host; he is named in the book *Zohar*, folio 137, the king of the angels. He is said to be called by the name Metatron, because that name has two significations which express his condition, namely, that he is a lord and a messenger. He is alleged to have been the conductor of Israel through the wilderness, and is frequently styled an angel, of whom God says, "My name is in him." He brought out the Israelites from Egypt; and he it is of whom it is said, in Mal. iii. 1: "And suddenly He shall come to His temple, the Lord whom ye seek, and the angel of the covenant, in whom ye delight, shall certainly come." According to the book *Tykune Zohar*, Metatron is a man in the image of God,—an emanation from God,—and this is Jehovah, of whom can be affirmed neither creation nor formation, but only emanation.

Concerning Evil Beings.

The rabbis differ in opinion concerning the origin of evil beings. Some say that they were once inhabitants of heaven, but they were cast out when they fell from their state of holiness and glory; and, according to some of them, this happened soon after the creation of Adam; or, as others think, in the days of Noah. But, according to many rabbis, they proceeded from the hands of their Creator, with all their present evil propensities. Certain rabbis affirm that the demons are made—some of fire, others of air, others of water and earth. Others declare them to be all composed of two elements—fire and air. But the Jews, generally, accept the opinion of the Talmud, which says, in the book *Chagiga*, fol. 16, c. 2 : "Six things are declared concerning demons : they have three things in common with ministering angels, and three things in common with men. They have wings, they fly from one extremity of the world to the other ; they know future events, like ministering angels ; they eat and drink ; propagate and multiply ; and they die, like men."

According to the Talmud tract, *Cholin*, fol. 105, c. 2, and *Zohar*, Emek Hammelech, Jalkut Rubeni, and Nishmath Chajim, some demons are described as having no power to do any great mischief, beyond delighting themselves with hoaxing men by various waggish tricks. Others are represented as polluting fountains and streams of water ; others as afflicting mankind with sudden and grievous distempers; and others, as doing various injuries to human beings while asleep. As some great Jewish authorities, as Rabbi Bechai and Jalkut Chadash, have it, none of the unclean powers will perish, but they will all be purified and made holy.

Concerning the Soul.

According to Jewish doctrine, the human body is animated with a triple soul, which is designated by the terms nephesh, ruach, and meshama. Rabbi Meir says, in *Abodath Hakkodesh*, fol. 4, c. 2 : "In man there is a nephesh and a ruach; and according to his good works he is made worthy of a higher glory in what is called the neshama. All are bound together, the nephesh to the ruach, the ruach to the neshama, and the neshama to the holy and blessed God." The *Tseror Hamaor*, fol. 3, c. 1, says: "God created three worlds—the upper, the middle, and the lower world;" and in connection with this it is said, in the book *Zohar*, "That God created three souls answering to the three worlds—namely, the nephish, that is the soul; and the ruach, which is the spirit; and the neshama, that is the precious soul. The nephish is created with a view to the middle world; but the neshama with regard to the upper world. Wherefore, by means of these three souls a man is qualified to inhabit the three worlds; and he abides sometimes in the lower, sometimes in the middle, sometimes in the upper world,—all of which happens according to his qualifications, and the qualifications of these souls. These three souls enter the body at distinct periods. According to the *Sepher Gilgulim*, the nephish enters at the birth of a man; the ruach, at the age of thirteen years and one day, if his deeds are right; and the neshama enters at the twentieth year, if his deeds continue to be right. But if, on the contrary, his deeds are not right, the nephish and ruach remain without the neshama. Sometimes a man is only worthy of the nephesh, and so continues without the ruach and the neshama; and these two remain concealed in a place known only to the holy and blessed God.

According to some Jewish doctors, as Jalkut Chadash, there are five distinct forms or parts, and names of the soul,—the nephesh, ruach, neshama, the chaja, and the jechida. These are received by man at the following seasons: on working days, between the feast and the increase of the moon, comes to him the nephesh; on the feast-day comes to him the ruach; on the day of atonement, the neshama; and on the Sabbath, the supernumerary soul, which is the mystery of chaja; and in the life to come he is made worthy to receive the jechida.

The metempsychosis doctrine, which is, that one soul animates several bodies in succession, has been adopted by the Jews in general for many ages, and is still believed and recognised in the following prayer offered every night before retiring to rest,—" Sovereign of the Universe! behold, I freely forgive and pardon every one who hath aggrieved or vexed me, or who hath injured me either in body, goods, honour, or anything belonging to me, whether by compulsion or choice, ignorantly or presumptuously, in word or deed, in this transitory state or in any former one."

Concerning the number of transmigrations performed by each soul, the rabbis do not agree; neither do they agree as to whether it is the whole soul that transmigrates, or merely a portion of it. According to some of them, the human soul is an emanative substance, capable of dividing itself, as the generality maintain, into three; but according to some, into thirteen individual subsistencies, in order that the defects of the first subsistency may be repaired and counterbalanced by the perfection of the others. Some rabbis say that the soul goes but into three bodies for transmigration, not reckoning in the number the time when she first enters the world in a human body; and this is what Elihu signified to Job when he said, as in Job xxxiii. 29, "Lo, all these things worketh God twice and thrice with man." Others say that the soul transmigrates into four bodies, and this is the mystery of the words in Exod. xx. 5, "Visiting the iniquity of the fathers upon the children, unto the third and fourth generation." There are also some opinions, that when sin has disordered the soul she may, in order to recover herself, be frequently removed from body to body, even up to a thousand times, as it is said in Ps. cv. 8, "The word which He commanded to a thousand generations." The reasons for transmigration of the soul are given by the rabbis as the following: The soul of man passes into other bodies, either because she hath not remained her period in the first body, or because the soul, having committed sin, and being not perfectly purified from it, but being clogged with the dust of her transgression cleaving to her as straw is clogged with clay, she cannot ascend to God, till, by being poured from one vessel into another she becomes light and clean, and is annexed to the upper spirits, through which, passing from one to another, she ascends to the place of her first residence, from which she descended into the world.

The Origin of Sin.

The Jews do not believe in original sin, but in *Jetser Hara*, a term that may be rendered "evil principle," which they represent as the internal cause of all sins that men commit. The rabbis differ in their accounts as to the origin of this evil principle, but it is generally believed by the Jews that the evil principle is born with a man, and grows with him all his days. Therefore, every morning they offer the following prayer: "Let it be willed before Thy presence, O Lord our God, and the God of our ancestors! that Thou mayest accustom us in Thy law, and make us steadfast in Thy commandments. Lead us not into error, transgression, iniquity, temptation, nor into scorn. Let not the evil spirit have power over us. Keep us from bad men, and bad companions. Join us with good spirits and good deeds. Humble our evil thoughts, to be subservient unto Thee. Grant us, this day and daily, to find favour, grace, and compassion in Thine eyes, and in the eyes of all our beholders. Bestow on us good grace. Blessed art Thou, O Lord! who bestowest good graces towards His people Israel."

The Atonement.

The doctrine of the Jews respecting the terms of acceptance with God is as follows: At the time when the Jews had the full enjoyment of the privileges of the Temple, the remission of sin was through the sacrifice and by virtue of certain expiations; and now forgiveness is to be obtained by prayer, contrition, and other means, as the reader will see by the following prayers: "Sovereign of the Universe! Thou didst appoint us to offer the daily sacrifice in its appointed time, and that the priests should officiate in their proper service, and the Levites at their desk, and the Israelites in their station. But, at present, on account of our sins, the Temple is laid waste, and the daily sacrifice hath ceased; for we have neither an officiating priest, nor a Levite at the desk, nor an Israelite at his station. But Thou hast said, the prayers of our lips shall be accepted as the offering of bulls. Therefore let it be acceptable before Thee, O Lord our God, and the God of our ancestors! that the prayers of our lips may be accounted, accepted, and esteemed before Thee, as if we had offered the daily sacrifice in its appointed time, and had stood in our station."

And at the end of every fast they say: "Sovereign of the Universe! it is clearly known unto Thee that whilst the holy temple was established, if a man sinned he brought an offering of which they only offered its fat and blood; yet didst Thou in Thine abundant mercy grant him pardon. But now, because of our iniquities, the holy temple is destroyed, and we have neither sanctuary nor priest to atone for us. O, may it therefore be acceptable in thy presence, that the diminution of my fat and blood, which hath been diminished this day, may be accounted as fat offered and placed on the altar, and thus be accepted of me."

Concerning Paradise.

The Jews believe in a twofold paradise—one above in heaven, and another here below upon earth. It is in the lower paradise that the righteous dwell during the week days. Between the upper and lower paradise is fixed a pillar by which they are joined together; it is called the strength of the hill of Zion. By this pillar, on every Sabbath and festival, the righteous climb up and feed themselves with a glance of the Divine Majesty till the end of the Sabbath or festival, when they slide down and return to the lower paradise.

The reader will perhaps be interested in the following tradition concerning paradise, as narrated in the Talmud, book *Chetuveth*, fol. 77.

"Rabbi Jehosha Ben Levi was a perfectly righteous man. Now, when the time of his departure from this world was at hand, the holy and blessed God said to the Angel of Death, 'Comply with all that he requires of thee.' Then said the angel to Jehosha, 'The time draweth nigh when thou art to depart from this world. I will grant thee all that thou requirest.' When Rabbi Jehosha heard this, he said to him, 'My request to thee is that thou wilt show me my place in paradise.' And the angel said to him, 'Come along with me; I will show it thee.' Whereupon Rabbi Jehosha said, 'Give me thy sword that thou mayest not therewith surprise me.' And immediately the Angel of Death gave him his sword; and they went together till they came to the walls of paradise. When they were come up to the walls, the Angel of Death raised Rabbi Jehosha up, and set him upon them. Then jumped Rabbi Jehosha Ben Levi from the walls, and descended into paradise. But the Angel of Death caught hold of the skirts of his cloak, and said to him, 'Do thou come out.' But Rabbi Jehosha did swear by the name of the Eternal God that he would not come out from thence; and the Angel of Death had not the power to enter in. Hereupon, the ministering angels presented themselves before God and said,

'Behold what the son of Levi has done; he has by force taken his part in paradise.' Then follows a conversation, which terminates in a decision that 'he shall not go out of paradise.' And the Angel of Death, seeing that he could not draw him out, said to him, 'Give me my sword.' But Rabbi Jehosha refused to give it him, till a voice came from heaven, which said, 'Give him the sword, for he has occasion for it for the killing of others therewith.' And Rabbi Jehosha said to him, 'Swear thou to me that thou wilt not let it be seen by man or any creature when thou takest away their souls.' For before that time the angel had been used to slay mankind, even the infant on the mother's lap, in a manner visible to all. And the Angel of Death did swear in that same hour, and Jehosha gave him his sword again. Then Elijah began to lift up his voice before Rabbi Jehosha, saying to the righteous, 'Make room for the son of Levi! make room for the son of Levi!'"

Traditions Concerning Hell.

According to Jewish tradition, hell, or as it is called in Hebrew, Gehinnom [the word Gehinnom is borrowed from the name of a valley near Jerusalem, where idolatrous Israelites sometimes sacrificed their children in the fire to Molech—2 Kings xxiii. 10], has seven names—hell, destruction, corruption, a horrible pit, the miry clay, the shadow of death, the nether parts of the earth. These names are said to be the appellations of seven sections or mansions into which hell is divided. Each of these names is assigned to a distinct abóde, and they are all together called Gehinnom. It is further stated that in hell there are seven dwellings or divisions, and in each division six thousand houses, and in each house six thousand chests, and in each chest six thousand barrels of gall. In each of these dwellings there are said to be seven rivers of fire, and seven rivers of hail, and many other terrible punishments, too numerous to mention. The different districts of hell are appointed for the infliction of different degrees of punishment. Each one is assigned to this or that dwelling, according as he has deserved; but it is believed that at each time of prayer—morning, afternoon, and night—they have an hour and a half of rest. So they rest, on the whole, every day four and a half hours. They likewise rest twenty-four hours on the Sabbath, which, added to the others, makes fifty-one hours of rest in the week.

Some rabbis are of the opinion that even most of the righteous are subject to the punishment of hell, in order to cleanse them from their stains; but hell has no power, even over the most sinful Israelite, to consume or destroy. The righteous go down to hell, only to be put into some emotion, and be frightened; but the sinful ones are scorched for their offences.

There is a medium of liberation for Israelites from hell, which is greatly prompted and accelerated by the following prayer of their surviving sons, and which must be said publicly every day, three times, during the first year after death :—" May His great name be magnified; may it be sanctified throughout the world which He hath created, according to His own good pleasure. May He establish His kingdom, while ye live, in your days, and while all the house of Israel be living, speedily, even time quickly coming; and say ye, Amen.

"May His great name be blessed; may it be adored for ever, even for ever and ever.

"May all blessings, praises, glorifying, exaltation, eminence, honour, excellence, and adoration be ascribed unto His holy and blessed name, far exceeding all blessings, hymns, praises, and beatitudes which are recited throughout the world; and say ye, Amen.

"May the supplications and entreaties of all the house of Israel be accepted in the presence of their Father, who is in heaven; and say ye, Amen.

"May there be abundance of peace from heaven, with life unto us and all Israel; and say ye, Amen.

"May the Maker of Peace, through His infinite mercies, grant peace unto us and to all Israel; and say ye, Amen."

This prayer, called Kadesh, is in the Aramaic language. The reason given by the Jews for this is, that the prayer is so grand and glorious that if the angels understood it, they would be jealous. Therefore it is arranged in a language that the angels cannot understand, as they know only the Hebrew language. But how these prayers, in which there is no mention of the dead, are to deliver them from purgatory, is a mystery even to the Jews themselves.

CHAPTER XXVIII.

JEWISH MARRIAGES—THEIR TRADITION AND CELEBRATION.

DURING the year in which I studied in Lubavitz, under the leader of the sect Chabad, I was harassed by the marriage-makers, who were very anxious that I should marry, notwithstanding that I was only seventeen years of age. Amongst the Jews, marriages are arranged by men who make it their profession. They find out who has a son or a daughter, and make it their business to bring the parents of both parties to an agreement. So the young people have nothing to say in the matter. However, in my case it was different, as my father was not alive, and my mother would not do anything without consulting my wishes. I certainly would have refused their proposals, as my love for study, and the determination to carry out my resolution of establishing a new Jewish sect, was so great, had it not been that marriage is accounted an indispensable duty of every Jew, and the proper time for discharging this duty is at the age of eighteen years. A Jew who lives single till the age of twenty is considered by his brethren as profligate. I therefore agreed to marry the daughter of a Jewish landowner, who was an eminent man of the Chabad sect.

The tradition concerning marriages is, that at the beginning of the world, souls were created by God in pairs, consisting each of a male and female; and therefore they affirm that marriage is either a reward or a punishment, according to the works which a man has done. For if a man is deserving and accounted worthy, he obtains his original consort; the person with whom he was created is bestowed upon him as a reward. But if otherwise, he is punished by being united to a person of uncongenial dispositions and manners, with whom he is doomed to live in almost continual strifes, contentions, and miseries.

When a marriage is agreed upon, the promise is made before witnesses, and a contract, which is called a contract of conditions, is written; two copies are made and delivered, one to each party. The parties remain betrothed, sometimes six months, sometimes a year, or more, before the marriage takes place. Occasionally the parents betroth their sons and daughters while they are still children, and sometimes they are even married at the age of fourteen.

The marriage is celebrated as follows: On the day fixed for the solemnisation of the nuptials, the bridegroom, if he reside in the same town as the bride, goes a couple of miles out from town with his relatives, in order that he may be brought in again with ceremony by the relatives of the bride, who go to meet him, and conduct him to the house of one of their friends. He is then visited by young men, who shake hands with him, saying *Shalom Alechem*, *i.e.*, "peace be unto you!" After these greetings, he is escorted, with music, to the bride. He throws a veil over her, and the witnesses say the blessing in Genesis xxiv. 60 : "Thou art our sister, be thou the mother of thousands of millions." The bridegroom puts on a surplice, over which he throws an overcoat, and is escorted, with ceremony, by men, to the canopy which is placed outside the synagogue. The bride follows immediately, escorted by her parents, upon whose arms she leans, and they are followed by a large company, including the most, or all of their friends and acquaintances. The bridegroom and bride are placed opposite each other, under the canopy, and the rabbi, or whoever performs the ceremony, takes a glass of wine in his hand, and pronounces the following blessings: " Blessed art Thou, O Lord our God, King of the Universe! the Creator of the fruit of the vine. Blessed art Thou, O Lord our God, King of the Universe! who hath sanctified us with His commandments, and hath forbid us fornication, and hath prohibited unto us the betrothed, but hath allowed unto us those that are married to us by means of the canopy and weddingring. Blessed art Thou, O Lord! Sanctifier of His people Israel, by the means of the canopy and wedlock." The bridegroom and the bride then drink of the wine, after which the bridegroom takes the ring, and puts it on the bride's finger, saying, " Behold thou art wedded to me with this ring, according to the law of Moses and Israel."

Then the marriage contract is read, which specifies that the bridegroom, A B, agrees to take the bride, C D, as his lawful wife, according to the law of Moses and Israel; and that he will keep, maintain, honour, and cherish her, according to the manner of all the Jews, who honour, keep, maintain, and cherish their wives; and that he will keep her in clothing decently, according to the custom of the world. This document also specifies what sum he settles upon her, in case of his death; and he obliges his heirs, executors, and administrators to pay the same to her out of the first produce of his effects.

After the reading of the marriage contract, the rabbi, or whoever the officiating person may be, takes another glass of wine, and repeats the following benediction: "Blessed art Thou, O Jehovah our God, King of the Universe! who hast created joy and gladness, bridegroom and bride, delight and song, pleasure and sympathy, love and brotherhood, peace and friendship. Speedily, O Jehovah our God! let there be heard in the cities of Judah, and in the streets of Jerusalem, the voice of joy and the voice of gladness, the voice of the bridegroom and the voice of the bride, the voice of the merriment of the bridegrooms from out of their canopies, and youths from their musical feasts. Blessed art Thou, O Jehovah! the rejoicer of the bridegroom with the bride."

The bridegroom and the bride then drink the wine; the empty glass is then laid on the ground, and the bridegroom, stamping on it, breaks it in pieces. This is done to indicate the frailty of life, or as a remembrance of the destruction of the temple, and is founded upon the sixth verse of Ps. cxxxvii.: "If I prefer not Jerusalem to my chief joy." Then all the company shout: *Mazol Touv*—*i.e.*, "good luck to you." The married pair are then escorted with ceremony to the house of the bride's parents, where they break their fast, which had lasted the whole day. The wedding feast is as sumptuous as the parties can afford, and continues for seven days. After the seven days of the wedding feast, the young couple remain with the parents of the bride and bridegroom alternately, and are supplied with every comfort which the parents are able to afford, for as many years as have been agreed upon by the parents of both parties at the time of their betrothal. The young man generally continues his studies in the Talmud for some years, and then, if he has sufficient ability, and is so inclined, and gets a congregation, he becomes a rabbi; if not, he becomes a merchant or a money-lender. Very often the women carry on the business while their husbands sit at home or in the synagogue reading the Talmud or other rabbinical books; and many women consider it an honour to have such pious husbands who do not care at all for worldly engagements.

CHAPTER XIX.

MY DISSATISFACTION WITH THE RELIGIOUS STATE OF THE JEWS; TRAVELLING FOR A YEAR IN RUSSIA, AND PREACHING WITH A VIEW TO REFORMATION AMONG THE JEWS; MY ACQUAINTANCE WITH THE SECT CALLED KARAITES, AND DISPUTE WITH THEIR CHIEF CHACHAM.

IN my home, where all pains were taken to make me comfortable, I was nevertheless unhappy, owing to an unsatisfied longing which filled my breast, to reform the Jewish communities, which, in my opinion, were not what they ought to be, for the following reasons:—

First, The belief that the Jews are selected from all other people because the Lord God loved them, and exalted them above all other nations, and sanctified them with His commandments, and chose them for His service, made me think that the Jews must occupy another position among the nations, and be no longer, as they are, a curse and a by-word among them.

Secondly, These thoughts led me to search the Scriptures, in order to find whether the Jews had ever fulfilled the duties for which they were called and chosen, namely, to proclaim the glorious kingdom of God to the whole world.

Thirdly, Do the Jews do anything in accordance

with the following prayer, which they repeat three times a day? "We do hope in Thee, O Jehovah our God! to behold speedily the glory of Thy power, to pass away the unworthy from the earth, and destroy their idols, that the universe may be established in the kingdom of the Almighty; for all the children of the creation shall call on Thy name, and all the wicked of the earth turn unto Thee, that they may know and acknowledge—all the inhabitants of the universe—that unto Thee shall every knee bend, and every tongue shall be satisfied. Before Thy presence, O Jehovah our God! they shall kneel and prostrate, and they shall give honour and glory unto Thy name, and they shall partake of the yoke of Thy kingdom, and speedily reign over them for ever and ever: for the kingdom is Thine, and for ever and ever Thou shalt reign in glory; as it is written in Thy law, the Lord shall reign for ever and ever."

Fourthly, How shall we be a real people of God, the children of His covenant, the offspring of Abraham His beloved, the seed of Isaac His only one, the community of Jacob whom the Lord loved, and called his name Israel and Jeshurun?

I came to the conclusion that the Jews must be stirred up and reformed, and I felt convinced that I had a call from God to do it. I therefore resolved to preach the following terms:—That all the Jews shall return to the Mosaic organisation, as it is in Exod. xviii. 25, 26; to have one leader under the supremacy of God, and an overseer over every thousand, hundred, fifty, and ten. The overseers shall be chosen by the people, according to Deut. i. 13, whose duty shall be to unite and advise the Jews to do the will of God, according to Deut. iv. 6 : "Keep therefore and do them; for this is your wisdom and your understanding in the sight of the nations, which shall hear all these statutes, and say, Surely this great nation is a wise and understanding people;" and to lay aside all things which are not for the glory of God.

Moreover, I resolved to visit various countries, and to make acquaintance with all the Jewish sects, and also to visit the Holy Land, in order to learn what is best for the prosperity of the Jews.

In the beginning of the year 1867, I undertook this great journey, and after I had visited a very large number of Jewish congregations in different towns, where I was received with great honour and preached with great success, I arrived in the Russian province, Crimea, where I made acquaintance with the Jewish sect, Karaites, *i.e.*, Scripturists, so called, because they are attached only to the Scriptures of the Old Testament, and not to the Talmud. I was delighted with them, as I had longed for many years to see them and could not, as there were none in my native province, their chief seat being in the Crimea, where they are in number about 30,000. They are also in small numbers in Lithuania, Constantinople, Damascus, Cairo, and a few in Palestine; their whole number will be about 50,000.

The Jews regard the Karaites in religious matters as the Roman Catholics do the Protestants, but in social life they look upon them as even worse than upon Christians. They do not intermarry, nor hold any intercourse with them. The Karaites had greater privileges in Russia than other Jews, probably because they are not so numerous and peculiar as the Talmudical Jews are.

The origin of the Karaites is disputable. They themselves say that they are the genuine successors of the Jewish Church, and that only they have preserved the true Jewish religion since the time of Ezra, the inspired scribe, and the great synagogue, and that the other Jews are gone astray through the doctrine of the rabbis. But the Jews reject these pretensions, and say that the Karaites are apostates, the successors of the Sadducees. The Sadducees were one of the Jewish sects before the destruction of Jerusalem, of whom Flavius Josephus, in the "Antiquities of the Jews" (book xviii. chap. i. sect. 1), writes:—That Judas and Sadduc excited a fourth philosophic sect among us, and had a great many followers therein, filled our civil government with tumults at present, and laid the foundation of our future miseries by this system of philosophy which we were before unacquainted withal; concerning which we shall discourse a little, and this the rather, because the infection which spread thence among the younger sort, who were zealous for it, brought the public to destruction." The period of the origin of the Karaites is not known, but it cannot be denied that they have subsisted for many centuries. From the gravestones which were found by the chief chacham, Abraham Firkowitz, in this century, it is evident that the Karaites were already, in the beginning of the first century, in the peninsula of the Crimea.

After I had visited several Karaite congregations

in different towns in the Crimea, I went to Bachsisarai, to meet the chief chacham of this sect, with whom I had a long dispute, as follows:—Our question was, "Who are the apostates, the Rabbinists or the Karaites?" The chacham was of the opinion that the Rabbinists are the apostates, because they added to the Mosaic law, another one which was not given by Moses on Mount Sinai; and more than that, they are attached more to the teaching of the Talmud than to the Bible; but the Karaites keep strictly to the law which the blessed God commanded to Moses, who was faithful in his house and faithfully delivered it, written, to the Jews.

"This is your apostasy," said I to the chacham, "that you do not believe that many things were delivered orally to Moses on Mount Sinai, which are not comprehended in the written law; and what you said you cannot believe in the Talmud, because it is not said there, as it is in the Bible, 'The Lord said unto Moses, saying,' but it is said 'Rabbi Jochanan says,' or 'Rabbi Akiba says,' but you can never find in it 'God said,'—that is simply because the Talmud was transmitted by oral tradition only, and at the period when the oral law was in danger of being forgotten, the wise men of that age (blessed be their memory!), committed to writing whatever each individual had received from his predecessor, and had put under his name, the name of 'who said' at that time, but it was the words of God which were delivered orally to Moses on Mount Sinai. If we had not the Talmud, we could not understand the written law, of which it gives explanations, and according to Deut. xvii. 11, we are commanded to do according to the word which our rabbis teach us."

"It is wrong of you Rabbinists to believe," replied the chacham, "that the books of Moses require an interpretation. We believe that every scripture brings with it its own interpretation; and it is most ridiculous to believe that God gave a written law which could not be understood without a verbal explanation, which He Himself had to give to Moses."

The chacham quoted so many passages from the Scriptures against the Talmud that I could not answer him; but as my pride would not give way, I made a long cabalistic speech, trying to explain that God had to give a written and an oral law; but the chacham declared that he did not believe in my explanation, and that my long speech was only a fantastic one. I became very excited, and said to him: "You are not only unbelievers in our holy traditions, but also in God, for you are the followers of the Sadducees." He then calmly took a Hebrew book, and handed it to me, saying: "Young rabbi, take and read our fundamental articles, and you will see that we have not the same belief as the Sadducees." I took the book and read the following articles:—

"1. That all material existencies, the worlds and all that are in them, are created.

"2. That the Creator of these things is Himself uncreated.

"3. That there is no similitude of Him, but that He is in every respect One alone.

"4. That Moses our master (peace to his memory!) was sent by Him.

" 5. That with and by Moses He sent us His perfect law.

" 6. That the faithful are bound to know the language of our law and its exposition; that is, the Scripture and its interpretation.

" 7. That the blessed God guided the other prophets by the prophetic spirit.

" 8. That the blessed God will restore the children of men to life at the day of judgment.

" 9. That the blessed God will render to every man according to his ways and the fruit of his doings.

" 10. That the blessed God has not rejected His people in captivity, even while under His chastisements; but it is proper that even every day they should receive their salvation by Messiah, the son of David."

We then further disputed for a long time, but could not come to an agreement. I left the chief of the Karaites, taking with me many of his views concerning the Jewish religion. Soon afterwards I left the province of the Crimea, to return home.

CHAPTER XX.

MY OCCUPYING THE OFFICE OF A RABBI DURING THE ILLNESS AND AFTER THE DEATH OF MY COUSIN; RELIGIOUS CEREMONIES CONNECTED WITH ILLNESS, DEATH, BURIAL, AND MOURNING; AND A STRANGE TALE CONNECTED WITH THE PRAYER FOR THE DEAD.

ON my way home I visited my cousin Jacob, who was a rabbi in Vierchneprovsk, and found him very ill. I was, therefore, urgently asked by him and his congregation to remain and perform his duty until he should recover. I complied; but his illness now became dangerous. The whole congregation came together to the synagogue, and after chanting some psalms, I read the following prayer, and changed the name Jacob to *Chaim* :—

"God be merciful unto Jacob, and restore him to life and wonted strength. Let his name henceforth be called *Chaim;* let him rejoice in this his name, and let it be confirmed upon him. Let it please Thee, O God! that this change of his name may annul all hard and evil decrees, and reverse the sentence which has been passed against him. If death has been decreed upon Jacob, it is not issued against Chaim. Behold, he is at this hour, as it were, another man—as a new creature, as an infant just born to a good life and length of days."

I had scarcely ended the prayer when a messenger arrived to tell me that the rabbi was dying. When I returned to his house I met two men at the door, who were carrying out all the water that was in the house to throw it away, it being customary among the Jews, when any one dies, to throw away instantly all the water in that house and in the three adjoining houses on either side; for this reason, the angel of death is supposed to wash his sword in the water, and make it unclean.

On entering the house I found my dead cousin already on the floor, for it is the custom among the Jews that, immediately on a person's decease, the dead body is stripped and laid on the floor upon clean straw, a pillow under the head, and a cover thrown over the body, lighted candles being placed at the head of the corpse. The body remains in that state, watched by one or two Jews, until the ceremony of cleansing with warm water is performed. Part of this ceremony consists in holding the body erect, and pouring over it three successive ablutions, accompanied by a recital of the following passage of Scripture in Hebrew, from Ezek. xxxvi. 25: "And I will sprinkle clean water upon you, and ye shall be clean from all your filthiness." After some hours the ceremony of washing was performed, and the rabbi was dressed in white garments, over which was put the talleth, *i.e.*, the square garment with the fringes, which the deceased had worn in the synagogue during prayers. The corpse was then laid on a bed, and carried in procession to the synagogue, where I delivered a funeral sermon, which consisted of an eulogy upon the deceased. Thence the procession proceeded to the burial-ground. The bed, resting on poles, was carried on the shoulders of various parties alternately, it being a great honour to carry it. It was set down seven times, while the elders and noble Jews of the congregation walked round it in procession repeating prayers. When they arrived at the grave, the relations and friends of the deceased rabbi, one after another, approached the corpse, holding one of his great toes in each hand, imploring him to forgive all the offences they had committed against him in his lifetime, and not to report evil of them in the other world. Four plain boards loosely joined like the sides of a box, but with no bottom, are fitted into the grave, and the body is laid between them. The Jews do not use close coffins, in order that the body may the sooner decay; for as long as it remains, it is supposed to suffer pain from worms. Thus the rabbi was interred by the chiefs of the congregation. Some earth, which was brought from the Holy Land, was thrown upon the corpse, and the so-called coffin was covered with a plain board. Those who stood near the grave then threw in some earth, and all present united in the following prayer: "He is the rock; His work is perfect, for all His ways are judgments; a God of truth, just and upright is He. He is the rock; He is perfect in all His work. Who is it that can say unto Him, What workest Thou? He governeth above and beneath; He killeth and maketh alive; He maketh to go down into the grave, and bringeth up again.

K

He is the rock; He is perfect in all His doings. Who is it can say unto Him, What doest Thou? He it is who speaks, and it is done; He works mercy unto us for nought, and for the merits of him who was bound as a lamb. Be attentive and do. He is righteous in all His ways; He is the rock; He is perfect, long-suffering, and full of mercy. O, have pity and compassion, we pray Thee, on the fathers and the children; for Thou art the Lord of forgiveness and mercy. Thou art righteous, O Lord! to kill and to make alive; for in Thy hands are deposited all the spirits. Far be it from Thee to blot out our remembrance, but let Thine eyes be upon us with mercy, for Thou art the Lord of mercy and forgiveness. Yea, if a man lives one year, or he lives a thousand years, what profit hath he? Behold, he is as though he had never been. Blessed be the true Judge who killeth and maketh alive; blessed be He, for His judgment is true, and He perceiveth all things with His eye, and pays unto man his reckoning and judgment, and all do give praise unto His name. We know, O Lord! that Thy judgment is just; Thou art justified with Thy words and the merits of Thy justice, and none can complain of the order of Thy justice. Righteous art Thou, O Lord! and upright is Thy judgment,—a true Judge, and judgest true. Blessed be the true Judge, for all His judgments are just and true. The souls of all living are in Thy power; justice filleth the right hand, and power. O have compassion on the remnant of the sheep of Thy hands, and say to the angel, Stay thy hand. Mighty in council and great in work; behold Thine eyes are open upon all the ways of the children of men, to give to every man according to his ways, and the fruit of his works. To show that the Lord is upright, He is my rock, and there is no unrighteousness in Him. The Lord gave and the Lord hath taken away, blessed be the name of the Lord! And He, being full of compassion, forgiveth iniquity, and doth not destroy; yea, frequently turneth away His anger, and doth not stir up all His wrath."

As soon as the grave was filled up, all present went away as fast as possible, lest they should hear the knock of the angel, who is supposed to come and knock upon the grave, saying in Hebrew, "Wicked! wicked! What is thy *pasuk?*" That the reader may know what this pasuk means, it is necessary to state that every Jew's name has a pasuk—*i.e.*, a verse of Scripture—attached to it, as for instance, to my name, Elieser, belongs the pasuk in Psalm xxii. 11—"Be not far from me, for trouble is near; for there is none to help." In Hebrew this verse commences with an א, *Aleph,* and ends with a ר, *Resh,* the first and last letters of the name; the intervening letters are also to be found in the verse. And so every Jewish name has a pasuk which he is taught as soon as he is able to speak. He repeats it in Hebrew every day, in order that he may be able to answer the angel when he comes to the grave. If he is not able to answer what his pasuk is, then it is said that the angel beats him with a hot iron till he breaks his bones.

Before leaving the burying-ground, it is customary amongst the Jews to pluck some grass and throw it behind, saying, "They shall spring forth from the city as the grass of the earth." They do not enter a house until they have washed their hands and said, "He will swallow up death for ever, and the Lord God will wipe away the tears from off all faces; and the rebuke of His people will be removed from off all the earth; for the Lord hath spoken it." They also repeat the 91st Psalm, beginning at the last verse of the 90th.

When we returned home from the funeral of my relative, those most nearly related to him sat down upon the floor according to the Jewish custom, and a low table was placed before them containing hard boiled eggs, some salt, and a small round loaf. Each took a small portion in order to break the fast which they professed to have kept from the moment of the decease. One of the greatest tokens of sorrow amongst the Jews for the death of their relatives is the rending of their garments. This is done as follows: On the decease of a brother or sister, wife, son, or daughter, they cut with a knife one of their garments, and then rend it about a handbreadth in length. On the decease of a father or mother, the rent is made in the same manner on the left side in all the garments. The second token of mourning is sitting on the floor without shoes, which they continue to do for seven days, during which time they neither go out nor transact any business. During these seven days, free access is allowed to every one, friend or stranger, for visiting the bereaved family. The third token is not to cut the nails, nor to take a bath for thirty days. For eleven months, the sons or nearest relatives of the deceased repeat three times a day the Kadesh—a prayer which is considered as having sufficient efficacy to deliver the deceased from hell. This prayer has to be repeated in the presence of no fewer than ten Jews, who have passed the age of thirteen. That the reader may have an idea how important and valued the Kadesh for the deceased is, I will introduce an anecdote which is believed among the Jews at large to be true.

"Rabbi Manasseh was travelling in Spain, and saw on a hill at a great distance a man with a bundle of sticks on his shoulder, who, through acquaintance with the *Cabala*, he knew to be dead. As the rabbi gazed, he saw the dead man take the sticks from his shoulder, strike a light by rubbing two pieces of wood together, kindle a fire, and lay himself down, when he was soon consumed to ashes. Then came the angel Gabriel with a broom in his hand and swept the ashes together, and from them the dead man arose to life; on which the rabbi asked him what he was guilty of while he lived, that he should have to go through such torments? He replied, 'I have now been dead twenty years; I was a most wicked Jew, doing everything vile except murder; and the moment I died, I was doomed to go day by day for a hundred years to collect sticks in a wood, to set them on fire, and to be consumed as you have seen this day. Twenty years of the time have expired, but, alas! eighty remain.' The rabbi rejoined, 'Is there no help for you in the lower world.' The dead man answered, 'Yes; I have a son living at Andalusia in Spain, and if he would say Kadesh I should be redeemed from my torments.' 'Then,' said the rabbi, 'why did not your son say

Kadesh, according to the Jewish custom?' The reply was, 'I was so dreadfully wicked that I did not deserve it; acting unkindly to my children while I sinned against God.' At this statement the rabbi promised to visit the son, and set out on his journey forthwith. After travelling many leagues, he entered a synagogue, and in the midst of the congregation inquired about the deceased people, and particularly the man who died twenty years ago; but the answer was, 'That he must not inquire as that person was very wicked, and his name should not be mentioned in the synagogue.' He told, however, what he had witnessed, and at length found out the son, who no sooner heard of his father's condition than his heart melted, though he stated that he had neglected to say Kadesh because his father had acted most wickedly to himself, his family, and his God. The rabbi entreated him to say Kadesh. That night he did so in the midst of the congregation; and between eleven and twelve the curtains of the rabbi were drawn aside, and the dead man appeared with one shining spot upon his body, and thus spoke: 'See the utility of saying Kadesh; the first my son uttered has delivered me from one year's torment, and every time he does so I shall have a year less to suffer.' The son was very diligent, and when he had said Kadesh the eightieth time the father appeared again to Rabbi Manasseh as a shining light, all glory, and kissed him, and said, 'Go and tell the Jews at large the importance of saying prayers for a departed spirit; now my soul is perfected, it will go into paradise, and my sins shall be thought of no more.'"

After the decease of my cousin, his congregation wished me to become their rabbi, though I was still very young; but this I refused, and remained only for a few weeks until another rabbi came, when I returned home.

CHAPTER XXI.

DISRUPTION OF THE SECT CHABAD; REASONS WHY I WAS CONSIDERED BY SOME JEWS AS A MIRACLE-PERFORMER; MY JOURNEY TO THE EAST; AND MY ACQUAINTANCE WITH THE MISSIONARIES IN CONSTANTINOPLE.

DURING the year of my travelling in Russia, a great change took place in the sect Chabad, to which I belonged. The leader of the sect, Rabbi Mendul Schnerson, died, and left six sons. In his will it was found that the youngest son, Rabbi Samuel, was appointed leader; but the orthodox Jews were not satisfied with the will, for they wished to have the second son, Rabbi Lion, for their leader. Hence arose a quarrel among the Chabad sect, and a disruption ensued. Rabbi Lion left Lubawitz, the residence of his father, at the urgent request of his party, and took up his residence in Kopest, a small town in the province of Mohilew. Rabbi Samuel remained in Lubawitz with his brethren, and the wealthy of his sect were his party.

Immediately upon my arrival at home, I went to Lubawitz to see the grave of my beloved Rabbi Mendul, and prayed there for some hours. I visited all his sons; but had no sympathy with any of them, as I found in none of them the spirit of their father. I therefore resolved to bring forward my new doctrine, which was a mixture of Rabbinism and Karaitism, and commenced preaching it very carefully. For four months I preached in my native province, and succeeded in obtaining some disciples, and especially those who considered me as a miracle-performer. Why I was so called will be seen from the following:—

At one time I visited a sick Jew, and gave to him some cabalistic remedies, which were as follows: Some almonds on which I wrote in Hebrew, אגלא—*i.e.*, initials of four Hebrew words, which signify in English, "Thou art ever strong, O Lord." He was to eat three almonds three times a day; and because the man recovered, it was considered that a miracle had been performed.

Another day I visited a poor man, who had been confined to bed for some days. I told him, before leaving, that I would call next day for him, and that he should accompany me to the synagogue. Accordingly, when I visited him on the following day, I found him dressed and waiting to go with me. The Jews who were assembled in the synagogue, and who knew that Benjamin had been ill, were amazed to see him come in with me, and thought that I performed a miracle. In this instance, as in the former, I also firmly believed that I had wrought a miracle; whereas, I now look upon it as quite natural. Both men had a firm belief that I was such a holy man that God would not deny my request, and this belief led them to exert themselves as above mentioned.

On another occasion I advised a Jew to deal in wax, at the same time giving him my blessing; and as he was successful, and soon made a fortune, it was considered that I had performed a miracle.

Many Jews used to come to me for advice, and a blessing on their business. Others requested me to pray for the healing of their sick. Others, again, desired spiritual counsel; and when I gave a blessing, or a cabalistic remedy, or any advice to a Jew, he, as well as myself, believed that I had power from God to do it.

However, I was not happy, and so I resolved to undertake a journey to Palestine, where I could examine the places connected with the Bible and with the Talmud, and so obtain a clearer view of everything, ascertain what I ought to do in connection with my new doctrine, and how to do it.

In July, 1868, I left my native place for the East, and visited many towns which I had not seen before. In Taganrog, where I arrived in August and remained for five weeks in order to take sea-bathing, I heard for the first time of missionaries. Taganrog is the town where the Emperor Alexander I. of Russia died, in 1825. It stands on a high promontory, near the north-eastern extremity of the Sea of Azof. The climate is temperate and remarkably healthy; and therefore I resolved to remain there, in order to recruit my health and enjoy the rest I was so much in need of. In the hotel I met with several Jews from Constantinople, and heard them speak of the missionaries there. I eagerly inquired what missionaries were, but could not obtain much information respecting them. I was told, "You will hear of them when you go to Constantinople."

From Taganrog I went to Kertch, a seaport town of Russia, which was celebrated as a stronghold against the Anglo-French expedition during the siege of Sebastopol, in 1854-55. I remained in Kertch during the Feast of Tabernacles, and preached several times with great success, and was requested to stay there as a preacher for some months, in order to stir up the Jews; but this I was unwilling to do, my object being to come first to a clear understanding with myself; for the many conversations I had had with infidels in Charkof, and Rostof, and Taganrog, had made some sceptical impressions upon me. I therefore resolved to observe very minutely every thing, every religious conversation, and every religious form with which I should become acquainted in my journey.

From Kertch I sailed by steamer to Odessa, the most flourishing seaport town of Russia, which is situated on the east of the Black Sea. I remained in Odessa for a few weeks; and here for the first time I indulged in worldly pursuits and pleasures. I there met with an intimate friend, who had formerly been my colleague in the Rabbinical Academy. We were greatly pleased to meet again; but I soon found that our religious views now widely differed, I remaining still a bigoted Jew, while he had become somewhat of a sceptic. I accompanied him to the theatre, for the first time in my life; but I did not understand much of it, as the play was in the Italian language. The next evening I declined to go with him, as I did not like it; but he persuaded me, saying the play would be in Russian, which I understood and would like. During my stay in Odessa, he drew my attention to many things of which I had not the slightest idea previously.

All this, however, did not really amuse me, for my religious studies were more precious to me than all the pleasures of this world. After spending an evening with my friend in the theatre, or in any other place of worldly amusement, I would go home and read nearly the whole night in the book *Zohar*, in order to purify my soul after being in unclean places.

In this town, also, I was sometimes cheated and robbed, and I made such experiences as I had never before dreamed of. There again I heard of the missionaries in Constantinople, but could obtain no more information than in Taganrog. But this I was told, that the son of the rabbi from Odessa, when he went for a visit to Constantinople, was caught in the missionaries' net.

Never in my life was I so tired of any place as of Odessa, and I left it with the impression that the man who spends his time in religious intercourse is much happier than he who lives in pursuit of worldly pleasures.

In the beginning of 1869, I found myself in the capital of the Ottoman Porte, where I was received with open arms by my Jewish co-religionists, who, perceiving my searching spirit, made it their first care to warn me of the missionaries, and to put me on my guard against their "insidious arts to entrap the unwary into Protestantism." An unconquerable feeling of curiosity arose within me. What are missionaries? What are Protestants? I asked myself. What kind of persons could they be of whom the Jews speak only with curses and anathemas? Puffed up with pride and conceit, and sure of victory in bringing them to see they were in error, I sought an interview with them.

My Jewish friends, in great alarm, endeavoured to dissuade me from running a risk so dangerous; but, despising all remonstrances, I determined to have my own way in the matter.

END OF PART I.

Part II.

THE HEBREW CHRISTIAN.

AN ACCOUNT OF HOW THE AUTHOR WAS PRIVILEGED, NOT ONLY TO BELIEVE IN CHRIST, BUT ALSO TO SUFFER FOR HIS SAKE, AND TO TESTIFY OF HIS GRACE TO JEWS AND GENTILES. ALSO, A GLIMPSE INTO THE CORRUPTION OF THE RUSSIAN GOVERNMENT OFFICIALS IN THE NINETEENTH CENTURY.

CHAPTER I.

MY ACQUAINTANCE WITH THE MISSIONARIES; A CONVERSATION CONCERNING THE MESSIAH; THE JEWISH HISTORY OF CHRIST; MY CONVERSION AND BAPTISM; A LETTER FROM REV. A. TOMORY TO THE JEWISH MISSION COMMITTEE; INTIMATION TO MY RELATIONS AND FRIENDS IN RUSSIA THAT I HAD FOUND THE EXPECTED MESSIAH; A LETTER FROM REV. A. TOMORY TO F. BROWN-DOUGLAS, ESQ.

ONE day in 1869, as I was standing outside the door of my lodgings, with the son of my host, I was rather startled, as a gentleman passed, to hear my companion suddenly exclaim, amidst a volley of abuse and execrations, "There goes that apostate who was once a teacher in our Jewish school, and now he has deserted us. We are all very sorry that he fell into the trap of the missionaries, for he was a pious Israelite, but through them he became a follower of the Crucified One."

His words made me very eager to speak to that apostate, and to learn from his own lips the reason of his falling into the snare of the missionaries. I immediately made an excuse for leaving my host so abruptly, and followed the young Protestant, whose name was Gutman, until he had passed the bounds of Galata, which is the Jewish quarter, that I might not be seen by the Jews, speaking to an apostate. When we came to Pera, I went up to Mr. Gutman, and inquired from him the way to the Russian Post. This I did in order to open a conversation with him. He evidently understood me at once, and asked if I was of Russia. On my answering in the affirmative, he said, "And what is heard there of the Messiah?" My answer was, "We believe in Russia, as all the Jews throughout the world, that the Messiah will come, and this is one of the articles of our faith, to believe in his coming, and 'to expect him every day.'"

I accompanied Mr. Gutman to the house of Rev. A. Tomory, then to Mr. Landsmann, with whom I had disputes for several hours each day. On the first day, as I left Mr. Landsmann, he gave me a copy of the New Testament in Hebrew, and I did not retire to rest until I had read it through. As it was the first time I had read this blessed book, it made upon me a very peculiar impression. I compared it with the book *Toldoth Jeshu, i.e.*, "the book of the generation of Jesus." This book was fabricated by unknown rabbis, who employed all the means which enmity and ingenuity could supply, to perpetuate and strengthen the prejudices of their nation against Christ. The book was published in Hebrew, with a Latin version, in the year 1681, together with a refutation by Wagenseil. For a long time the Jews were exceedingly careful to conceal this book from the eyes of Christians; and since copies have been obtained by Christians, and published to the world and refuted, the Jews in general disowned it. But manuscripts in Hebrew are universally circulated among the Jews, and more than that, Jewish children are taught it like nursery rhymes, and thus grow up with prejudice against the historical relations of the gospels, very difficult to eradicate from the Jewish mind. They who have ever spoken to a Jew concerning the history of Christ, must have heard the reply, "You believe what is said in the gospels, but we know the real history of Jesus better."

After I had finished reading the New Testament I retired to bed, but as I could get no rest, I got up and paced my room, comparing the history of Christ, as I read it in the gospels, with that which was rooted in my mind. I said to myself that both described Jesus as one who performed various miracles. According to the Gospel by John, he worked those miracles because the fulness of the Godhead dwelt in him, but according to the Jewish history, he accomplished them by the virtue of *Shemhamphorash*, or "the ineffable name of God." I could not come to any conclusion, and therefore went next morning very early to the missionaries, and had again a conversation with them, which lasted for several hours. On my return home, I searched the Bible with great earnestness, comparing scripture with scripture, and every day I went to the missionaries, disputing with them for several hours. At last I came to the knowledge that the Messiah has indeed come, and that Jesus is the Messiah, according to Moses and the prophets. An especial impression was made upon me by the tenth verse of the forty-ninth chapter of Genesis. "The sceptre shall not depart from Judah, nor a lawgiver from between his feet, until Shiloh come; and unto him shall the gathering of the people be." A great change took place in me after my conversations with the missionaries. My natural pride seemed to fly from me; all my fancied holiness and righteousness appeared as filthy rags; I felt the need of a Saviour, but could not, as yet, accept Christ in my heart. My knowledge of Him was only that of the understanding. I could draw near to Him with my mouth, but my heart was far from Him. To the missionaries I unbosomed my spiritual trouble, and told them I should be happy if I could receive Christ into my heart, as I had received Him into my understanding. They replied that they could instruct me about Christ from the Scriptures, but that He could only come into my heart when I opened it to Him in earnest prayer, for we have the promise of God that He is near to all who call upon Him in truth. I went home and entreated the Lord, with tears, to show me the truth, whether Jesus was really the Messiah, and if He were, then to give me love to Him. The gracious Saviour had compassion on me, and revealed Himself to me, as He does to all those who come to Him in faith. He gave me love, hope, and trust, and I yielded myself entirely to God's guidance. I asked Mr. Tomory to instruct me in the Christian doctrine.

After about ten weeks, under his teaching, I was baptised in the Mission Chapel, 19th April, 1869, in the presence of a large congregation of Jews and Christians.

That the reader may have an idea of my spiritual state at that time, I think it well to give a letter, from the Rev. Alexander Tomory to F. Brown-Douglas, Esq., which was published in the *Free Church Record*, June, 1869.

"CONSTANTINOPLE, 26th April, 1869.

"Elieser was baptised last Sabbath, the 19th of April. It was a peculiarly interesting occasion. His baptism created such a stir in the Jewish community that our place of worship was crowded in every part with Jews.

"The leadings of the Lord with his soul were remarkable from the beginning, and we trust the Lord will perfect in mercy all that concerneth him. The Lord drew him, and taught him, and baptised him with the heavenly baptism; the time of his inquiry was a time of overflowing mercy. It was one continuous stream of life and light that the Lord seemed to send into this frail vessel—he could often scarcely bear it. And yet he was not spared the sighings and cryings. One night his pleadings were nearly as follows: 'Thou wilt by no means cast out those that come unto Thee. Here I am, I cannot go away till Thou receivest me in covenant love.'

"These words he repeated again and again in Hebrew, and a gracious God heard him. When he rose from his knees, he felt an assurance that only the spirit of adoption can give. He is a renewed, happy, saved soul. His history is one of a revival here. We trust he will be spared, and prepared to be a living witness for the truth.

"The history and the conversion of this man may really be an encouragement to committees, to societies, and to all the friends of Israel. Verily there is a remnant according to the election of grace. The time to favour Zion seems truly near.

"I asked Dr. Thomson to administer baptism to him.

With the Doctor, although he is many years now out of Jewish work, it is still the Jew first; and I knew he would consider it a gratification and a privilege to administer baptism to such a convert. My text was from John i. 46 : 'Come and see.' The crowd listened very attentively; and a young man, who is only here for a few days, called yesterday and said: 'The words "Come and see" ring in my ears; I wish to hear more.' He has means, and he is down in the Home, listening to the Word of Life. Remember us in your prayers. Next Sabbath we have our half-yearly communion, and Elieser will be among the company."

The day of my baptism was to me a day of rejoicing and victory, and the following few weeks were the happiest time of my life; for I did not and could not see what lay before me in the future. Nor did I then know that the words which the Lord spake of Saul of Tarsus, "I will show him how great things he must suffer for my name's sake," were spoken also to me. It was during this happy time that I wrote to my relations, and to my former instructors and colleagues, telling them that I had found our expected Messiah in Jesus of Nazareth. I thought it my duty to acquaint my friends in Russia with the step I had taken, and I did it with great joy, in the hope that some of them would also be saved through my feeble instrumentality.

CHAPTER II.

MY FIRST ZEAL IN PREACHING THE GOSPEL; MY SEVERE ILLNESS; ENGAGEMENT AS TEACHER IN THE MISSION SCHOOL; ARRIVAL OF A JEWISH DEPUTY FROM RUSSIA TO CONFER WITH ME; BY BRIBERY OF JEWISH GOLD I WAS MADE PRISONER, AND CONVEYED ON BOARD A RUSSIAN VESSEL TO ODESSA; EXTRACT FROM THE "FREE CHURCH RECORD" OF DECEMBER, 1869.

AFTER my baptism, I could no longer refrain from proclaiming the Gospel to my Jewish brethren; and although Mr. Tomory advised me not to go to the Jewish quarter for a time, lest the Jews should be violent with me, I could not help going and preaching to them in the streets of Constantinople. The rabbi invited me to his house; and in company with Mr. Landsmann I went there, and expounded the truth of the Gospel, not only to the rabbi, but to a number of Jews who were present. The rabbi told us that he had written to my family, to inform them of the step I had taken, and of the disgrace I had brought upon them and upon the Jews in Constantinople, who had received me with great kindness and honour on my arrival in the Ottoman Empire.

The excitement and agitations of the past few months were not without effect on my physical frame;

and in a short time after my baptism I was laid low with a severe attack of typhus fever, which for some weeks threatened to bring me to the grave. But I was very happy, having no fear of death. On the contrary, I would gladly have departed, to be with Christ, if such had been the Lord's will; but He willed that I should abide in the flesh, to testify of His grace and mercy. I slowly recovered; and as soon as my health and strength returned, I entered, on 29th September, with great alacrity and much prayer, upon my work in the Mission School, and was full of joy at the opportunity of serving the Lord in such a good cause. Little, however, did I or any member of the mission dream of what was before me.

The reader will remember that, in the foregoing chapter, I mentioned that, directly after my baptism, I intimated to my relations and friends in Russia that I had found the expected Messiah, and that Jesus was He, and I was become His disciple; and I told them that if they wished to be saved they must accept Him, for He is the Angel who is spoken of in Job xxxiii. 23, 24. Every letter contained many proofs from Moses and the prophets that the Messiah has come, and that Jesus is the expected son of David of whom the Psalmist speaks, Ps. cx.: "The Lord said unto my Lord, Sit Thou at my right hand until I make Thine enemies Thy footstool." With these letters my relatives and friends went to the chief rabbi, to whom I had also written a letter. A solemn council was held, and a resolution passed that a deputy should be sent to Constantinople to confer with me, and persuade me to return with him to Russia. This deputy, who was one of my nearest relatives, arrived about the middle of June; but as I was seriously ill at that time, he did not present himself either to me or to any of the Mission for a few weeks, until I became better. From our first interview, he and the rabbis used their utmost endeavours to induce me to give up my faith in Christ. But finding that all their efforts were unsuccessful, they turned in bitter anger, and took a solemn oath not to leave unturned any stone until they had succeeded in removing me from Constantinople; thinking that in Russia they would be able to force me to return to Judaism. They did not delay to carry out their intentions.

I shall never be able to forget the 2nd of October, 1869, nor the grace of God in giving us spiritual food to strengthen us for the hour of trial. On that morning, when I visited the Rev. A. Tomory, neither he nor I dreaming that it would be the last time of seeing each other under his roof, nor thinking in the least what was about to happen, we read together the eighth chapter of the Epistle to the Romans, the last five verses of which especially comforted me greatly from that day to the present time. After reading and prayer, I returned home. In the afternoon the deputy visited me, and found me studying geography, with a large map before me. He asked me to show him where Mohilew was, and when I did so, he said that he hoped one day to see me there. He then requested me to take a walk with him in the fresh air, that we might have some conversation, adding that he was very anxious to learn all he could about Christ. Full of joy with the thought of such a change in him, who was recently so bitterly opposed to Christ and His doctrine, I gladly agreed to accompany him, and thus embrace the opportunity of explaining to him the loving kindness of our Redeemer.

Scarcely, however, had we reached the open street of Galata, when I was seized by a Russian policeman, dragged before the Russian consul, and lodged in the prison of the Russian chancery on the plea that I had left Russia in order to escape the military conscription. In vain I pleaded that I was now a Turkish rajah, that I had one brother in the army, and therefore, according to Russian law, it was optional to me to enter military service. All my representations, as well as those of my Christian friends, were of no avail, for Jewish gold was very potent, and the officials had been bribed therewith. Accordingly, the Russian consul expressed his determination to send me to Russia, in the Odessa steamer, on Tuesday the 5th of October.

I think it will be interesting to the reader, if I give an extract from a letter of Mr. Tomory, which appeared in the *Free Church Record* of December, 1869: "Who knows how much they have spent besides in bribery to be able to carry out so successfully such a daring act of seizing an innocent man in the open street of Constantinople, to be shipped off to Russia, there to be condemned to go to Siberia, or to the mines, or to a perpetual dungeon. We applied at once to the native Protestant chancery, and the Porte asked the restoration of its subject, seized in this unlawful and violent manner. I applied also to the Russian consul, to induce him, by a statement of the facts, to set Elieser at liberty. We got other Christian friends of influence and standing to take the matter in hand. They tried to arrest the man in his daring act of religious persecution, but it was all in vain. On the 5th October, the poor man was sent off to Odessa. He felt happy and cheerful. All the members of the Mission were permitted to go on board, and to take leave of him. We recommended him to God and to the word of His grace. Elieser will, by the grace of God, adorn the doctrine of the Gospel, and witness a good confession wherever he goes. He carries with him a firm faith and a martyr's spirit. His interview with the Russian consul here, and the answers he gave him, remind one of Paul before Festus and Agrippa; but it would be a pity if such a man should be allowed, through neglect, to rot in a dungeon. We feel it a duty to do what we can for his liberation. I sent a female member of our congregation to Odessa—a kind Phœbe. She is from there, and knows all the ways of that land of bribery and tyranny. Dr. Schauffler wrote to a very influential man there. The Reformed pastor and other Christian brethren have promised to do their utmost, that the governor-general, upon whom perhaps the whole issue depends, may do him justice. Elieser is a victim of persecution, but he has done nothing. His elder brother serves in the army, and this exempts him, according to Russian law. He is of weakly constitution, and quite unfit for military service. We have therefore good hope for his restoration. May the Lord bless the means, and hear in mercy our supplications. Heavy as these tidings are, the whole tale is not yet told. While the policeman was taking

Elieser to prison, they passed by Selinger's shop. The former called to him to come to his rescue. Selinger merely laid his hand on the arm of the policeman, and said, 'What right have you to apprehend him, he being a Turkish subject?' But the policeman was bribed, and he brought against him a false charge, and Selinger was put into prison, and threatened with a lengthened confinement. All our applications for his release failed, and we felt that it depended upon the goodwill of our persecutor to release him. If spoken to in a friendly way, he might waive his right of punishing him, and pardon him. But who was to undertake the task? I could not go, because he was angry against me that I applied to the British authorities. I set out on Friday morning to seek some friend who would undertake that errand of love. Miss Whittet, at the same time, made up her mind to go herself to the consul, and intercede with him in behalf of the prisoner, and he actually gave her the promise; and when, a few minutes later, the Prussian chaplain called on him—whom I had sent—he said, 'I have promised to the English lady that the prisoner should be released next morning.' Selinger was liberated after five days' confinement, and rejoices to have been found worthy of suffering shame for Christ's sake."

CHAPTER III.

THE JEWISH TRIUMPH; MY ANSWER TO THEIR TRIUMPH; THE TERRIBLE NIGHT; THE TEMPTER; HELP AND STRENGTH FROM THE LORD.

THE reader has already seen from the letter in the foregoing chapter that I was conveyed a prisoner on board a Russian vessel, which was to set out in the afternoon of 5th October for Odessa, and that all the members of the mission were permitted to go on board to take leave of me. A little before the hour of separation my relative and several other Jews, the chief of my persecutors, came on board with great triumph at having got me into their power. The members of the Mission quitted the steamer with tears and sobs, which at such a painful parting could not be restrained. One Christian friend remained to accompany me to Odessa.

Very soon after this farewell from my friends, the vessel left the Bosphorus. My relative, who had maintained a long silence, at length approached me, and said, "Now I know that the God of Israel is the only true God, and that our great rabbi can perform miracles. When I went to Constantinople, the rabbi of Lubawitz gave me his blessing, and assured me that I should certainly bring you home again; and moreover, you would return to the Jewish religion. One of his assurances is now in fulfilment, and I have no doubt that the other, of bringing you back from your errors, will also be fulfilled." I replied as follows to his triumph, that he should not deceive himself, "The reason why my Saviour permitted me to fall into your hands, is that He has some wise purpose which I do not yet know; but He has not forsaken me, and in due time He will deliver me from your cruelty. Concerning your faith in the rabbi, that he will reclaim me from my errors, I must say that he himself is in error in not following the teaching of Moses and the prophets; how, then, will he be able to convince me that Christianity is false, and Talmudism true?"

The night was coming on, and my persecutors, finding they could make no impression upon me, retired to their berths. But another and greater tempter attacked me. As I paced the deck, hardly knowing what I was doing, my past life rushed before my mind; the thought of my large circle of relatives and friends whom I must give up, and of the torments and indignities to which I had been subjected by my Jewish brethren, and of the separation from my Christian friends, came upon me with such force that I was overwhelmed with anguish of mind and bitter sorrow. Whilst thus reflecting, I heard the voice of an unseen being whispering in my ear: "Unhappy man! unhappy man! bethink thyself of thy position; thou art entirely in the hands of the Jews; they will conduct thee to thy native place, and as thou art a too sincere follower of Christ, thou wilt but excite the anger and contempt of thy relations and former co-religionists, so that thy life will be in danger; there is nothing better for thee than to get rid of thy present miserable condition by casting thyself into the sea, leaving the consequences of it faithfully to thy Master. Either He will miraculously rescue thee, as in olden times He did the prophet Jonah, or He will take thy spirit to dwell with Him for ever. The Jews, with their miracle-performing rabbi, will be filled with shame and remorse, for the world will be loud in condemning the conduct of those Jews who are triumphing over thee."

The reader can perhaps imagine how I was half maddened by this suggestion, and was about to jump into the roaring waters, when an invisible hand restrained me, and a passage which I had read on the 2nd October with Mr. Tomory, a few hours before my seizure, came to my mind and brought me light; the words are in the Epistle to the Romans, viii. 35-39: "Who shall separate us from the love of Christ? shall tribulation, or distress, or persecution, or famine, or nakedness, or peril, or sword? As it is written, For Thy sake we are killed all the day long; we are accounted as sheep for the slaughter. Nay, in all these things we are more than conquerors through Him that loved us. For I am persuaded that neither death, nor life, nor angels, nor principalities, nor powers, nor things present, nor things to come; nor height, nor depth, nor any other creature, shall be able to separate us from the love of God, which is in Christ Jesus our Lord."

Immediately I threw myself on my knees, and thanked the Lord for the light He had sent me, and I implored Him not to leave me alone for a moment, for I was not able to fight with the tempter of souls.

Oh, how much we have to praise our heavenly Father for manifesting His Son, that He might destroy the works of the devil; and if we ask our blessed Lord for help, and trust in Him, we shall never be confounded. May the Lord help us to put our trust in Him fully at all times.

The following days I passed in conversing with my Christian friend, but mostly in speaking to the Jews of the love of God and His Son, Jesus Christ.

We arrived at Odessa on 7th October about noon; I was handed over by the captain of the vessel to the officers of the custom-house, and was sent from there to the office of the governor-general; but unfortunately the governor was out of town. I was therefore conducted to the chief officer of the town, who seemed to have heard something of my misfortunes; for he received me with the utmost politeness, which was quite unusual for a Russian official, and leading me into his private room, he asked me to be seated, and at his request, I told him how I became a Christian. I drew my Bible from my pocket, and pointed out the passages which led me to believe in Christ. As I read them to him I observed his face become grave, and I said to him: "I trust that these words are precious to your excellency, as they are to me;" and in the ardour of my love to Christ, I told him, with animation, of the love of God which we receive through Christ. The officer sat silent while I spoke; then he quitted the room with the words, "I will see what I can do for you."

During this interview, many Jews had assembled in the adjoining room, and the officer went in to them. I waited for two hours hoping for my release, but instead of a messenger of liberty a Cossack at length entered the room, and bade me follow him at once. Without knowing where he was going to take me, I obeyed the mandate. When in the street, I inquired where he had orders to take me to. He replied, "To the temporary prison." I then requested him to accompany me to a restaurant, as I wished some refreshment. He readily assented, knowing that he would receive a fee from me for doing so. Whilst I was taking my repast he drank glass after glass of wodka, *i.e.*, whisky, so that I could easily have escaped from him, but I waited for the Lord's time to be set free; and instead of the Cossack conducting me to the prison, I had to take him, though not without great difficulty. However, we both arrived, and I was locked up in a filthy apartment with several prisoners. Scarcely was the door closed, when they surrounded me, and asked me where I came from. On my replying from Constantinople, they hastened to search my pockets, which, however, had already been rifled by an official before I was locked in the prison. I spoke solemnly to them in the words of the Apostle, "'Silver and gold have I none, but such as I have, give I thee.' I have better things to give you than silver or gold." "What is it?" they inquired, at the same time squeezing my cheeks to see if I had perhaps precious stones concealed in my mouth; for one of them said if I came from Constantinople, I must have precious stones with me, and as they were not in my pockets they must be in my mouth. But I replied, "I have no precious stones, but something much better." "What is it?" exclaimed they, impatiently. "I will show you a way of escape from the punishment of your guilt." With coarse laughter they glanced at the barred window, then at the door, as if to assure me of the impossibility of escape. Some of them looked inquiringly at me, as if thinking that I possessed some magic power. I told them that I spoke not of escape from temporal punishment but from everlasting condemnation. Some of them, touched by my words, asked me if there were any hope for them who were guilty of terrible crimes? Yes, I said; and then told them the narrative of the thief upon the cross, and that Christ was ready to receive them when they repented, for He came into the world to save penitent sinners. For some hours I spoke to these criminals, they quietly listening; then I prayed with them, and my words were to them as water on the thirsty ground. I spoke, and they listened, until I fell asleep on the prison floor.

CHAPTER IV.

MY FIRST VISITORS IN PRISON BRING ME GOOD TIDINGS; MY SECOND VISITORS COME WITH THREATENINGS; MY REMOVAL TO THE COMMON PRISON; I AM TAKEN TO CONFER WITH THE RABBI; I DISPUTE WITH HIM IN THE PRESENCE OF MANY JEWS; THE KINDNESS OF THE RABBI TO ME; MY REMOVAL FROM ODESSA TO BALTA.

OCTOBER 8th, 1869.—My first visitors in the prison were the Christian friend who had accompanied me from Constantinople, and two more from Odessa, who brought me the glad intelligence that there was great hope of my being soon liberated. They told me of the applications to the authorities which had been made, both by the Christian friends in Constantinople and those in Odessa. Though I found comfort in the thought of so many friends who were praying and working for my liberation, I was not over sanguine, knowing by experience how easy it is to bribe a Russian official, and how diligent the Jews are in doing so.

Scarcely had these friends left me with the bright dream of freedom, when a second party of visitors arrived, consisting of my relative and several Jews, who informed that only two courses lay open to me: either entirely to renounce the Christian faith, in which case I should be restored to liberty, honour, and wealth for all the days of my life; or to be imprisoned for the remainder of my life. Moved by the Spirit of the Lord, I addressed them earnestly, and with steadfast resolution, and explained to them that the happiness or sufferings here below, are nothing when we compare them with the everlasting glory or misery; and I concluded with the words: "My Saviour has released me once and for ever, and no jail can imprison me, for my soul is free from everlasting bondage, and the Lord is with me, even here in this filthy prison, and where He is, there is light, happiness, and freedom.' The party then left, nor did they visit me again until I was removed from that prison.

Two days afterwards I was removed to the common prison, where hundreds of prisoners were together and could converse with each other. Some of them were imprisoned because they had no passports, others because they had neglected to renew those they had; others were murderers and criminals of the deepest dye. All there have one lot—they have but little food, and that little of the worst quality.

My relative and Jewish friends, anticipating that these hardships would break my spirit, determined to try once more if it were possible to win me back to my former faith; and with this view they bribed the Government officials to summon me to meet them at the house of one of the rabbis. Accompanied by two armed soldiers, I was one day escorted through the streets of Odessa, like some criminal, to the rabbi's house, where my relative and several other Jews awaited me. The rabbi greeted me kindly, and entered into a long dispute, reasoning with me in the most affectionate manner for some hours, while I calmly answered all his arguments. The Jews, however, who were present could not be calm, and finding they could not answer my arguments, they became angry and were ready to strike me; but the soldiers, who had been charged to bring me safely back to the prison, hastened to conduct me thither. I believe the Lord ordered that I should be thus escorted by soldiers, that they might protect me from the violence of the Jews; for I am sure that, but for such protection, they would have torn me in pieces.

The next day I was again brought before the rabbi, who received me with even greater friendliness than on the preceding day. Instead, however, of renewing his arguments with me, he led me into an adjoining room, and taking me by the hand, he said: "My son, I will not dispute further with you, for I fear God, and am convinced that you are an honest man. I can see that your belief is founded on the Word of God, and I envy your earnest faith." "Dear rabbi!" I exclaimed, "if you admire and envy my creed, why do you not adopt it?" "Oh, no," replied he, with a mournful shake of the head, "the religious belief which I have so long professed is too deeply rooted to be easily changed. Besides, I could never adopt Christianity, though at heart I am not opposed to it. God is merciful, and He has said 'the just shall live by His faith,' and if we each live up to our own convictions, and honestly follow them out, He will have mercy upon us in the last day." When I began to argue that there is only one way to be saved, and that one through the free grace of Christ, the rabbi, who was anxious to change the subject, interrupted me by inviting me to take tea with him. I was touched by his kindness, for I had expected to find in him a bitter opponent. He took my hand and led me to the table where his family was assembled. The time passed quickly, bringing me to the hour for my departure to the prison. With tears, the rabbi and his family bade me farewell; and the rabbi put a parcel of provisions into my hand with these words: "I know that in prison you suffer severely from hunger; you must, therefore, accept these few things which my wife has put up for you, and as for myself I will do my best to procure your release." To the soldiers who escorted me, he gave some kopeks to buy wodka with.

I had hardly entered the prison with my parcel when the prisoners surrounded me, seized my provisions, and divided them among themselves. I then addressed them, and they listened for more than an hour while I spoke of the bread of life, which Christ provides for all who put their trust in Him; and when I had finished my address, and offered up a prayer, they all folded their hands and solemnly bowed their heads. Great privileges were accorded me in that time of proclaiming the Word of God to many murderers who were on their way to Siberia. Twice a-week a transport was made of those prisoners who were condemned for life to the mines; and as they were brought to that prison for a day's rest from their march, I seized the opportunity of preaching to them the Gospel, of which they had never before heard; and I believe many were saved through my feeble instrumentality.

During the time of my imprisonment in Odessa, my relative was bribing the officials to transport me to my native place in the west of Russia. Accordingly, I was one morning conducted, about eight o'clock, with a large number of my fellow-prisoners into the prison yard, where we were chained together in couples, and then three or four of these couples attached behind each other by a long chain, as is the custom in Russia when transporting prisoners from place to place. Some hundreds of people had assembled to witness the departure of the transport, and amongst them many of my enemies and some Christian friends. I was coupled to a Jew, who, preferring to be chained to me rather than to one of the criminals, earnestly begged the commander of the transport for this favour. This unfortunate man was being taken to Balta, for having been bold enough to say to the chief of the police that he would let him have nothing more from his shop, until he had paid what he already owed to him. The Jew was sent to Balta, his native place, by the high official who had arrested him.

The roll having been called over, the mournful procession proceeded to the railway station. We marched in a long line, our chains clanking at every step; a number of soldiers with loaded arms guarded us. I was at first depressed in spirit, but soon found comfort by casting my burden on the Lord, feeling assured that He would always be with me and sustain me. Several Christian friends in Odessa, hearing of my misfortune, had assembled on the platform at the station to take leave of me and bid me God-speed. Among them was the old Christian friend who had accompanied me from Constantinople, and others who had visited me in the prison. They were all very sorrowful, saying, with tears, how much it pained them to see me suffering such trials. I consoled them with the assurance that it was for some good purpose that God permitted me to be thus dealt with; for I believe I had already been favoured by the Lord in being privileged to direct many of the prisoners to Christ. And who can tell how many more may hear the Word of God, and thereby be led to Christ through my feeble efforts! I then addressed the Jews, who had assembled to see the transport, from the carriage windows; and as the signal was given, and the train was slowly leaving the station, I observed the Christian friends speaking with great energy to the Jews.

While the train was speeding rapidly along, I commenced to preach the Gospel to my fellow-prisoners; and the commander of the transport, seeing me with the Bible in my hand referring to various passages, was surprised at so unusual a proceeding, and entered into conversation with me. On hearing the details of my unjust imprisonment, he immediately unlocked my chains, and I was free to proclaim the tidings of redeeming grace to my companions until the evening, when we arrived in Balta, and were once more lodged in the town prison.

CHAPTER V.

FOUR DAYS IN THE PRISON AT BALTA; FROM BALTA TO OLWIOPOL; A WEEK'S IMPRISONMENT; FROM OLWIOPOL TO UMAN; ADDRESS TO THE PEASANTS.

THE four days of my confinement in the prison at Balta seemed to me to pass very rapidly, as I spent them in preaching the Gospel of Christ to Jews and Gentiles in the prison. The Jews residing in the town visited me daily, more, however, to abuse me than anything else, for the Jews in Odessa had acquainted them with my religious views, and had stirred them up against me. But the Jews in the prison heard me gladly. They said, "We listen to you willingly, for you speak to us from the convictions of your inmost heart,—and what comes from the heart goes to the heart."

At the end of the four days my chains, which had been temporarily removed, were again put upon me, and I was conveyed, with a transport of prisoners, to Olwiopol. We journeyed for two days on foot, passing the intervening night in a peasant's house which had been prepared for us. The dirty floor, however, was our only bed; and as the chains were not taken off from us, if one moved or turned himself in sleep, he disturbed the rest, who were enjoying a sound sleep after the weary march of the day.

On our arrival at Olwiopol a crowd of Jews, who had been informed of my coming, was assembled near the prison eager to see me; but their curiosity was not long gratified, for we were marched straightway to the jail, where also several Jews were imprisoned. Even they had previously received intelligence of my coming, consequently I was regarded by some of them with suspicion. Others requested me to explain the new doctrines I had embraced; but by the majority of them, Jews and Gentiles, I was mocked and jeered at, maltreated, and spit upon. I bore this bad treatment without a murmur, looking to our great Master, who submitted Himself to all kinds of indignities. One day when I was preaching in the prison yard, and telling the prisoners that they were all sinners, and that unless they would repent and seek forgiveness through Christ, they would perish eternally, they became so enraged with me that some of them struck me in the face; but raising my eyes to heaven, I exclaimed aloud, in the words of our blessed Redeemer, "Father, forgive them!" These words touched them, and, after a moment's silence, I lifted up my voice in prayer for them. No sooner had I finished than several of them came up to me and, with tears, entreated my forgiveness.

After a week thus spent in the prison at Olwiopol, I was chained to a Russian convict, and, accompanied by three soldiers, renewed our fatiguing march. Towards evening we reached a village, where we were lodged for the night in a miserable house kept for the purpose of giving a night's shelter to prisoners on their transport from Olwiopol to Uman. The peasants who saw us as we passed the village had compassion on us and brought us food, for which I thanked them, and seized the opportunity of speaking to them on the words of our Lord (Matt. x. 42): "And whosoever shall give to drink unto one of these little ones a cup of cold water only, in the name of a disciple, verily, I say unto you, he shall in no wise lose his reward." The peasants were so delighted with my address that in a short time nearly the whole village—men, women, and children— came to hear me; and as the room was too small to admit them, I went out to them into the yard and preached for several hours to a crowded audience of eager and attentive listeners. When I concluded many came up to me imploring my blessing, and bestowing on me such titles as "saint," "prophet," &c.; and it was with great difficulty that I could persuade them that I was but a sinner like every human being, and that I was only saved by the free grace of Christ through believing in Him,—that He alone is able to save us. The next morning these kind-hearted, simple villagers brought a large waggon, drawn by oxen, for the accommodation of myself and my fellow-prisoner, and the three soldiers, and they also accompanied us as far as the village where we were to pass the next night. On our arrival there these good folks went and stirred up the peasants, and again I had the privilege of preaching the Gospel to a large number of eager listeners.

At an early hour on the next day we reached an inn kept by a rich Jew, famed for his hospitality, especially towards his own nation. The guards were aware of this, and they knew also that if they told him I was a Jewish rabbi, he would give them money to be kind to me. They accordingly asked me to tell the innkeeper that I was a Jewish rabbi. Referring to the Word of God, I replied firmly, "I cannot do it; for the Lord Jesus said, 'Whoso denieth Me before men, him will I also deny before my Father which is in heaven.'" The soldiers, however, not caring for the Lord or His Word, became angry with me, and told the Jew that I was a rabbi. No sooner did the landlord hear this than he hastened towards me, and, embracing me affectionately, bade me welcome to his house. Thanking him for his courtesy, I said: "I am not now what you take me to be; I am *Isch Meschichi*"—i.e., a Christian. With great surprise, and not quite understanding me, he said, "What! are you our expected Messiah?" "No," I replied; "but I am a follower of the Messiah." I then proceeded to show him, from Moses and the prophets, that the Messiah was already come, and Jesus is He. The bigoted Jew listened with polite indifference, and then turned away. Although he now knew who I was, he nevertheless sent me some food.

Towards evening, we arrived at another village, where, as usual, we had to rest upon a dirty floor; and towards the close of the following day, the fourth of our march from Olwiopol, we reached Uman, and were incarcerated in the town prison. The Jews confined in that jail for various offences appeared to be kindly disposed towards me, though they soon discovered that I was a Christian. One young man, in particular, seemed attracted by the Gospel I was preaching to them. These prisoners supplied me with food from their private stores, furnished to them by their friends in town. During the two days I was kept in that prison I had a very good opportunity of proclaiming to both Jews and nominal Christians the Word of God which leads to salvation; and I trust that some souls were gained for Christ. In heaven we shall know.

The reader would like to hear what the Christian friends were doing for me during the time that I was being marched from prison to prison. I cannot satisfy them better than by quoting the following few words from the *Free Church Record* of January, 1870:—
"Our readers will be anxious to know what has become of Elieser, the Christian Jew, who was so unceremoniously arrested in Galata. Mr. Tomory writes that he has good hopes of his speedy release. The friend in Odessa who was first communicated with has secured the good offices of Mr. Dalton, the pastor of the Reformed German Church in St. Petersburg; and through him the Dutch ambassador at the Russian Court has been so thoroughly interested in the case that we may now confidently anticipate a happy issue out of the trouble. This, however, does not lessen our dissatisfaction with the apparently defenceless state of our Jewish converts in the Turkish dominions."

CHAPTER VI.

FURTHER TROUBLES; I AM UNABLE TO PROCEED; A FEW DAYS' REST IN THE HOSPITAL AT WINNAGRODCA; OUR MARCH RENEWED; ARRIVAL AT KIEV; INTERVIEW WITH MY UNCLE; HIS FRUITLESS EFFORTS TO MAKE ME TURN FROM CHRISTIANITY; INWARD CONFLICTS AND FINAL VICTORY; A VISIT IN PRISON FROM MY UNCLE AND OTHER JEWS.

YOU have now seen, dear reader, what trials I had to undergo for Christ's sake; but they were nothing in comparison with those which awaited me.

After two days' imprisonment at Uman, I was chained to three murderers, and we were conducted to Winnagrodca. The roads had been rendered almost impassable by heavy rains and floods; the weather also was very cold and wet. I was weakened by want of food, and by the troubles I had already passed through, and my feet were wounded and bleeding; so that I was unable to proceed at the rapid pace of the guards, and I often stumbled. This was very annoying to my companions, for, being chained together, I dragged them with me, thus not only increasing their pain, but causing them to trample upon me. They frequently endeavoured to drag me along by the chains, while the soldiers beat me most unmercifully with the butt-end of their guns, not believing that I was really unable to walk. At last I sank powerless to the ground, at the same time crying out, "Lord Jesus, have mercy upon me!" The soldiers, after a short consultation among themselves, decided to separate me from the other prisoners, and to place me upon a peasant's waggon that happened to be at hand. In this way they conveyed me for a few miles, till we arrived at our night quarters. I was unconscious during the whole of that night. The next morning a conveyance was brought, and I was placed carefully upon it, so as to continue the journey to the next town, Winnagrodca, where I was placed in the prison hospital until I should get better.

After a few days' rest, I was again chained to other prisoners, and conducted on foot to Tarashza, a three days' march. There I was kept for two days, in the jail; and then, in company with more prisoners, the march was continued to Washilkow, where another two days' imprisonment was my lot. After this we proceeded on foot to Kiev, one of the oldest towns in Russia, and one which the Russians consider as a holy town, it being the first which embraced Christianity in the year 980, in the reign of the Grand Duke Vladimir.

In the prisons, as in the villages, I had great opportunities, every day, of proclaiming the Gospel of Christ to many who had never heard it. The fame of my preaching spread rapidly, so that before we reached a village the peasants had assembled, awaiting our arrival. At one place the villagers came up to me, embraced me with tears, and said: "Ah, dear brother, the Lord help thee to glorify His holy name, as thou hast done hitherto!"

On our arrival in Kiev, I was met by my uncle, a wealthy Jew, who, as soon as he saw me, sprang from his carriage, and came towards me, flinging himself upon my neck, and greeting me with the utmost affection. His first words were: "My beloved Elieser, thou hast plunged our whole house into mourning. Thou wast the crown and the glory of our family; now thou hast trampled it under foot. Thou hast forsaken our most holy religion for that of the Nazarene. I implore thee, my son, to give up this freak, and all the past shall be ignored and forgiven. Thy chains shall be removed, and whatsoever thy heart desires, thou shalt possess; only acknowledge thy errors, and God and man will pardon thee." In the first moment, my bodily sufferings during the past weeks of my persecution,—my future, which lay hidden before me, and—if I now refused my uncle's offer— a probable cruel death passed before my mind; but at once, as if moved by a spirit from above, I exclaimed with energy: "Dear uncle, none of the inducements that you hold out to me will ever separate me from the love of Christ. What shall it profit me, if I gain the whole world and lose my own soul? Show me, if you can, a better way of obtaining remission of my sins and the forgiveness of God, and I will gladly walk in it. But you cannot. You can only offer me temporal advantages, which God has permitted you to enjoy for a limited season, ere death deprives you of them. Tell me, dear uncle, have you the assurance of everlasting life, in the possession of this world's riches? Have you peace, when the thought of death comes to your mind? Surely not! But if you will look to the Messiah, for whose sake I suffer, and of whom Moses and the prophets spake, you will there find rest for your soul."

My uncle became very angry, and said: "Hold thy tongue! I cannot dispute with thee; but I ask thee either to renounce Christianity, or to take the consequences of thine obstinacy." With great firmness I replied: "I shall not deny my Saviour, who gave His life for me, that I might have eternal life." My uncle immediately took his seat in his carriage and drove away.

I was led into the office of the police court, where the Government officials, who had been handsomely bribed by my uncle, insisted that I should renounce my religious errors, as they called them, and return to the Jewish faith. On hearing this from the mouth of those professing to be Christians, I could not be silent, and in a tone that pierced to their very souls I cried: "What! you call yourselves Christians! You perhaps think also that you are children of God! No, surely not; you are the children of Satan! Alas! woe, woe is me! The holy name of Jesus is blasphemed through such hypocrites as you are. What will you answer in the last dread day of judgment, before the righteous Judge, the King of heaven and earth?" The officials stood petrified while I was speaking, and then they hurried away, one by one, as quickly as they could, without a word; and a little while afterwards I was taken to the common prison, where I remained for more than two weeks.

On the following day my uncle, accompanied by several learned Talmudical and rabbinical Jews, visited me, in order to have a controversy with me on the disputes which exist between Jews and Christians. We continued our discussions for some hours; and as I think the reader would like to know something of the proofs I gave, that we Christians are right in saying that the Messiah has come, I will give an extract from that controversy.

CHAPTER VII.

A DISPUTE WITH MY UNCLE AND OTHER JEWS, WHO VISITED ME IN THE PRISON OF KIEV, AS TO WHETHER THE MESSIAH HAS ALREADY COME, AND IF JESUS BE HE; AN ATTEMPT ON MY LIFE BY THE PRISONERS.

THE dispute between my visitors and myself, which I mentioned in the foregoing chapter, was at first a fierce and angry one; but I calmly replied to them: "If you really wish to prove to me that I am in error, you must first quietly hear my arguments, that you may know how to deal with me." To this they agreed; whereupon I began with a passage which had made a great impression upon my mind when I disputed with the missionaries in Constantinople. It was from Gen. xlix. 10: "The sceptre shall not depart from Judah, nor a lawgiver from between his feet, until Shiloh come." The word שבט, *shoevet*, sceptre, signifies a rod or staff of any kind; and particularly the rod or staff which belonged to each tribe, as an ensign of their authority. What is here meant is, that such authority as Judah then had, was to remain with his posterity; that is, that he should not cease from being a tribe, or body politic, having rulers and governors of his own, until a specified period. The word מחוקק, *mechokek*—*i.e.*, lawgiver—

signifies not only one who makes laws, but also one who exercises jurisdiction; the meaning is, there should not be wanting a judge of the race and posterity of Judah, until the time foretold—namely, when Shiloh should come. Shiloh is the Messiah; for, howsoever the word be explained, whether it signify, as the Targum of Onkelos explains: "Until the Messiah comes, whose is the kingdom;" or, as the Jerusalem Targum proposes, a word שׁיל, "a child," founded upon שליתה, "her young one," in Deut. xxviii. 27, and interprets שילה as "his (Judah's) child;" or, as some others explained, "the peacemaker,"—one thing, however, is certain, that all the ancient interpreters refer openly or tacitly to some individual Prince who was to come of Judah's line, and is called the Messiah. In early times the tribe of Judah was as conspicuous as any other. The second king of Israel was of the tribe of Judah; and from that time to the Babylonish captivity, Judah held the sceptre not only of a tribe, but of a kingdom. When it was promised that the sceptre should not depart from Judah, it was implied that it should depart from the other tribes; accordingly, the tribe of Benjamin became an appendage to the kingdom of Judah, and the other ten tribes were carried into Assyria, whence they never returned.

My uncle here interrupted me, saying: "The sceptre departed from Judah, through Nebuchadnezzar, as it did from the ten tribes, through Shalmanessar, king of Assyria."

"Well," I replied, "the tribes of Judah and Benjamin were also carried captive to Babylon, as the other ten tribes were to Assyria, but they returned after seventy years."

"But," said my uncle, "the sceptre departed from Judah for seventy years, and there is no difference between Judah and the departing of it from the ten tribes."

"Not so, my dear uncle," said I, "there is a great difference between the captivity of the ten tribes and that of Judah. Judah and Benjamin, during their captivity, lived as a distinct people, they had rulers and governors of their own, and a prince of Judah (Ezra i. 8.) These princes and rulers had the management of their return to Palestine, and of their settlement there. After their return from Babylon, they were under the dominion of the Persians, Greeks, and Romans, and not free as before the captivity, but still were a distinct people under their own laws, though their rulers and governors were subservient to these foreign masters; and afterwards under the Asmoneans and King Herod, and even in the time of Jesus, Judah's royalty was not departed. The ten tribes, however, are altogether lost in captivity. A wrested sceptre of Judah, a foreign yoke, were the preludes to the first advent of Shiloh; and since the coming of the Messiah, the monarchy of Israel is hopelessly lost, and about seventy years after the appearance of the Messiah in the world, Jerusalem was taken, the temple destroyed, and they themselves were either slain with the sword or sold for slaves. From that time they have never been as one body, or people, but have been dispersed among all nations, and have lived without a ruler, without a lawgiver, and without supreme authority and government in any part of the earth. This captivity has lasted not only for seventy years, but for eighteen hundred. We must therefore confess that Shiloh, who is the Messiah, has come, and that Jesus is He."

One of the Jews, who had heard me with respectful attention, now asked, "If the tribe of Judah were not lost in the Babylonish captivity, as the other ten tribes were in Assyria, because it was to remain till the coming of the Messiah, how is it that it is not lost after the appearance of Jesus?"

"Yes, dear friend," said I, "it is wonderful to think that the tribe of Judah still remains. Judah alone gives a name to the whole nation. That honour was given to Judah because out of him Shiloh came, and that honour shall remain until Israel shall return and seek the Lord their God and David their king (Hos. iii. 5). And He is the Messiah, and is often called by the name of David in the prophets, as the person in whom all the promises made to David were to be fulfilled. This King David of whom the Prophet Hosea speaks, is none other than Jesus Christ, the true Shepherd of Israel, to whom the name of David is given by the prophets, and acknowledged by Himself in the Gospel, and who has fulfilled all the duties of that office. The Scriptures call the Messiah David, because He was born of David after the flesh. He is the true heir and successor of David, a king for ever. He came into the world at the time prophesied by Jacob (Gen. xlix. 10), and not only for the Jews but for all nations, as Jacob saith: 'Unto Him shall the gathering of the people be.' The fulfilment of this prophecy commenced in the case of Cornelius the Centurion (Acts x.), and in a few years from that time the Gospel was disseminated over the most important parts of the then known world. And now we see how many millions of the Gentiles have become Christians. Again in Haggai ii. 7-10, we read that the Messiah will come to the second temple, not for the Jews only, but for all nations. 'The desire of all nations shall come.' Christ, who is the desire of all nations, as the Redeemer of the world, and the Guide and Director of mankind in the performance of their duty, shall come under the roof of this house; and though there is not the cloud of glory overshadowing the mercy-seat, which was a symbol of the Divine presence peculiar to Solomon's temple, it shall behold a much greater glory, even the presence of the Messiah, in whom shall dwell all the fulness of the Godhead bodily. The expectation, the hope, the desire of all nations, and of Israel in particular, rested on some person, of whom this description, delivered to us in the days of Abraham (Gen. xxii. 18) was handed down from one prophet to another, until, after the captivity, it rested upon the Messiah, whom the Jews about Jesus' time associated with the prophecy of Haggai,—that to the second temple, the Messiah, the hope of Israel, the blessing of Abraham should come. Then in Zech. vi. 12, 13, we see in the person of Joshua, the high priest, a type or representation of the Man, whose name is the BRANCH—namely, the Messiah. The passage will not answer to any other, but to Him, who was at once both King and Priest, and who, by uniting both characters in Himself, was perfectly qualified to bring about 'the counsel of peace,' or reconciliation between God and Man. 'Even He shall build the temple of the Lord.' He, the self-same Person, who should build the temple of Jehovah, not of stones, but a spiritual house, which is the Church of Christ, even He should have the honour of governing and presiding in it, in the capacities of both King and Priest, advancing the peace and prosperity of His people. Also (Mal. iii. 1), 'The Lord whom ye seek shall suddenly come to His temple, even the messenger of the covenant whom ye delight in: behold He shall come, saith the Lord of Hosts.' There is hardly a Jew, ancient or modern, who does not regard 'the Lord' in this text, as the Messiah. The temple, in the writings of a Jewish prophet, cannot be otherwise understood than literally to mean the temple of Jerusalem. Of this temple, therefore, the Person who is to come is expressly called 'the Lord.' The lord of any temple is, in the language of all writers, and in the natural meaning of the phrase, the divinity to whose worship it is consecrated. To no other divinity was the temple of Jerusalem consecrated than to the true and everlasting God, the Lord Jehovah, the Maker of heaven and earth. Here, then, we have the express testimony of Malachi, that the Messiah, the Deliverer, whose coming he announces, was no other than the Jehovah of the Old Testament; Jehovah, who had delivered the Israelites from Egyptian bondage, was to come in person to His temple, to effect the greater and more general deliverance, of which the former was but an imperfect type. The time of His coming is said to be 'suddenly, to His temple.' In accordance with this, the temple was the scene of our Lord's public ministry at Jerusalem. There He daily taught the people; there He held, frequently, disputations with the unbelieving scribes, Sadducees, and Pharisees. But there are three particular passages in His life, in which this prophecy seems to have been more remarkably fulfilled. The first is recorded in John ii. 13-16; the second, in John vii. 37-40; the third, in Matt. xxi. 1-13. In one and in all, but chiefly in the last of these three incidents, did Jesus of Nazareth, in His own person display, and in His conduct claim, the first and greatest character of the Messiah, foretold and described by all the preceding Jewish prophets, as well as by Malachi, 'the Lord coming to His temple.'

"As Jesus of Nazareth was 'the Lord' of the Jews' temple, so also was He 'the messenger of the covenant' foretold by Jeremiah (xxxi. 30-33), and by Ezekiel (xxxiv. 23-25, xxxvii. 24-27). That covenant was to be different from the Mosaic; it was to be general, for all nations; everlasting, for all ages; a law, written in the hearts of the faithful; the covenant which Jesus, as God's messenger, propounded generally to all nations, and which, in its own terms, is fitted to be everlasting, for all ages, and is a law written in the heart. Assuredly, then, Jesus of Nazareth was the messenger of the covenant, foretold by the Prophets Jeremiah and Ezekiel.

"More remarkably still has been fulfilled in Jesus of Nazareth the prophecy of Dan. ix. 24-27, where we read that Daniel, by examining the prophecy of Jeremiah, had discovered that the seventy years of the captivity had nearly expired; and here the angel reveals to him another period of time, importing that Jerusalem, after its restoration, should continue for a space of seventy times seven years, at the expiration of which it should be finally destroyed. By putting a week for seven years, 490 years are here reckoned from the time that the dispersed Jews should be brought to the holy city, and remain in it till the end of the 490 years. Towards the end of this period the Messiah will come, in order that the transgression should be finished and sin ended, iniquity be expiated, and everlasting righteousness brought in. From the seventh year of Artaxerxes Longimanus, when Ezra returned with a body of Jews from captivity, and revived the Jewish worship, and by the king's commission created magistrates in all the land to judge and govern the people according to the laws of God and of the king, (Ezra vii. 26), to the destruction of the city, was 490 years.

"Daniel prophesies further, that after sixty-two out of the seventy foregoing weeks, the Messiah shall be cut off. The Hebrew word כרת, is by the Jewish rabbis interpreted as the death inflicted by the sentence of a judge, which interpretation they confirm by the use of the expression in Lev. xvii. 14, and in 1 Sam. xxviii. 9. The Messiah was put to death, but 'not for Himself.' He, the just, suffered for us, the unjust. He was cut off by a voluntary suffering for the sins of all mankind, and by His resurrection triumphed as a prince over death, and over all His and our enemies. All the circumstances of His life are comprehended in this final event, when all things that were written of Him were accomplished. It was owing to the prophecy of Daniel concerning the seventy weeks, or 490 years, that the coming of the Messiah towards the end of the period, was generally expected among the nations of the East.

"Therefore, my dear brethren, let us, by keeping this in remembrance, regulate our thoughts, and compose our minds, and soften our hearts, mortify our passions, and fix our affections on Him who loved us, and for our sakes fasted, mourned, and wept, lived poor and died forsaken. Let us come to Jesus Christ, who is the desire of all nations, as it is written in Haggai ii. 7. We must, one and all, desire to have Him for our only Saviour and Redeemer, our only Mediator and Advocate. We must desire to have Him in all the offices which He has undertaken for us as our Prophet, our King, and our Priest; our Prophet to reveal His and our Father's will to us and in us; our King to rule and govern our hearts and affections, to keep both our souls and bodies in subjection; and our Priest, to make atonement for our sins, and thereby reconcile God to us and us to God."

One of the Jewish hearers observed: "According to your explanation, the Messiah was already come before the destruction of Jerusalem. Then, where is He now?"

I answered: "The 110th Psalm tells us where He is. 'The Lord (God the Father) said unto my Lord (God the Son, the Messiah), sit Thou at my right hand, until I make Thine enemies Thy footstool.' This regal power and glory were given to Christ only. And but of Jesus only are to be understood, in the diviner sense, the words of the 8th Psalm, namely,

That he is a man of mean appearance outwardly, not worthy to be considered or regarded by God; and who for the space of thirty-three years was subjected to a condition inferior to that of God. But then, after His sufferings in our flesh, He was raised by God with honour to the highest dignities, was made the supreme Ruler of heaven and earth: and all His enemies, and all His and His Church's persecutors were, and will be subjected to Him."

My uncle here interrupted me, saying: "But it is now more than eighteen hundred years since, and the enemies of Jesus are not yet put under Him."

"Well," I said, "we do not indeed see all things actually so subjected to the government of Jesus. There are many rebellious enemies of Christ who do rise up against him; but it is enough that He has taken possession of His glory, and He has put many millions under Him, and will in His own time subdue all the adverse powers. We now see that in Jesus Christ is fulfilled the prophecy of Isaiah v. 26: 'And He shall lift up an ensign to the nations;' and Isa. xi. 10: 'There shall be a root of Jesse which shall stand for an ensign of the people; to it shall the Gentiles seek; and His rest shall be glorious.' In Jesus Christ also is fulfilled the prophecy (Isa. lii. 15), 'He shall sprinkle many nations." This means, He shall purify whole nations by His blood, and present them holy to God. Like Moses (Exod. xxiv. 8) when he had given to the people of Israel the law, written on two tables of stone, He 'took the blood (of the burnt and peace-offerings), and sprinkled it on the people, and said, Behold the blood of the covenant, which the Lord made with you concerning all these words." By the blood of burnt-offerings and peace-offerings, was the first covenant between God and Israel confirmed; by the offering of the Messiah of Himself, was the new covenant made with all nations; and He put the law in their inward parts, and wrote it in their hearts. The blood of the covenant of Moses was a figure of the blood of Christ. So when we read in Isa. lii. 15, 'Kings shall shut their mouth at him,' we see that it was fulfilled in Jesus, because, out of respect, or fear of Jesus Christ, Gentile kings keep silence; and those kings and nations are instructed in such heavenly truth as human reason could never be able to discover; and they to whom no prophets were sent, or promise made of a Saviour, shall consider and receive His doctrine."

My uncle could restrain himself no longer, and being unable to answer my arguments, he broke forth in a torrent of abuse, and at last, rising from his seat, and shaking his fists at me, with the words, "Apostate! traitor! dog! we will resort to more stringent measures to force thee to return to the religion thou hast so basely forsaken," he left the room followed by his companions.

I was then removed from the visitors' room to the prisoners', where my companions were some of the most infamous characters that could be met with. Their profane, impious language so pained me, that I could not keep silence, although I was tired from the hot discourse with my visitors. I commenced remonstrating with them from the Word of God; but they became enraged, and rushed upon me, intending to put an end to my life. Providence, however, interposed and frustrated their wicked designs. The jailer, who was passing the room at that moment, hearing the noise, hastened to discover the cause of it. He found me lying, half unconscious, on the stone floor, wounded, bruised, and bleeding. With the assistance of the warders, I was carried to the prison hospital, where I remained for about a fortnight.

CHAPTER VIII.

HOW MY SUFFERINGS AWAKENED THE PITY OF SOME JEWS, WHO SOUGHT TO OBTAIN MY RELEASE; PERSECUTION BY MY UNCLE; FATIGUING MARCH FROM KIEV; A PECULIAR MEETING WITH A FORMER FELLOW-STUDENT OF A RABBINICAL COLLEGE; A STRANGE RUSSIAN CUSTOM FOR ASSISTING THE DEAD TO ENTER HEAVEN; IMPRISONMENT OF A JEWISH FAMILY ON ACCOUNT OF THE BAPTISM OF ONE OF THE MEMBERS; RUSSIAN PROVERBS.

MY sufferings in general, and those I had to endure in the prison of Kiev in particular, made such an impression on the Jews of that city, that many of the rich amongst them, who had before sided against me, endeavoured now to obtain my release. My uncle, who was hardened to all human kindness, induced the police, by means of large bribes, to send me away at once from Kiev, because he was afraid that many would rise up to procure my liberation, for the sake of common humanity.

About the end of November, when the snow fell thick and fast, the frost was intense and the wind bitterly cold, I was compelled to undertake a new march on foot, and chained to other prisoners. The miseries of chains, hunger, fatigue, and insufficient protection from the severity of the weather, made my walking so difficult that the soldiers had often to raise me from the ground to continue my miserable journey. On one of these occasions I was so exhausted that I fell powerless to the ground, and as the soldiers were unable to drag me further, one of their number went in haste to the small town which was a short distance from where I was lying in an unconscious state, in order to secure a waggon to convey me thither.

The party of prisoners, with the guards, continued their journey, and the two soldiers who remained with me collected all the fuel they could, and kindling a large fire, they put me near it. Meanwhile the other soldier, after procuring a waggon, returned, accompanied by many inhabitants of the town, amongst whom I afterwards recognised the Jewish rabbi, who had formerly been my colleague, and who had neither seen nor heard of me for some time. All seemed prompted by the feeling of curiosity, which the soldier had evidently raised by his peculiar intelligence of me. With the mass of people came also a doctor, who made me swallow some drops, which had the effect of opening my eyes. Whereupon the rabbi, who had been earnestly regarding me the whole time, gave a violent start, exclaiming, " Can it possibly be Elieser ? " He again examined my countenance, then addressed me : " Dear brother ! what has befallen thee ? Art thou really Elieser, or do my senses deceive me, and do I behold another ? "

His kindly voice aroused me, and raising myself I gazed into my friend's face, and we, at the same moment, recognised each other. The young rabbi burst into tears, seeing my pitiable condition, and with the assistance of the soldiers, he put me into the waggon, and I was conveyed to the town. He watched by my side all night, and the next day accompanied me a short distance on my weary journey. I embraced this opportunity, as much as my weakness permitted, to explain to him the reason of my suffering, and something of the doctrines of Christianity. He was deeply moved, and wept bitterly because he was unable to do anything to procure my release. His heart, which otherwise might have been steeled against a follower of Christ, was touched to the very core. He procured me nourishment as much as I could carry with me. I was very much strengthened by his sympathy and affection, and this enabled me for the next few days to continue my journey with less painfulness and weariness than heretofore.

One day, as our large party of prisoners were in march, we beheld a table on the road-side, loaded with good and substantial food, and when we reached the place we were all invited to partake of as much as we pleased. I was surprised, and demanded the meaning of this strange act of hospitality, which was soon explained. A wealthy Russian had recently lost his son by death, and, anxious to procure his speedy release from purgatory and admission into paradise, he spread a bountiful table for the prisoners who pass that village twice a week, hoping by this act to obtain quickly the much-coveted boon.

On hearing this I would not partake of anything, though I was suffering from hunger, and had such a good opportunity of appeasing it. The bereaved father seeing this, came forward and asked me the reason. "If," said he, "it is because you are a Jew, there are plenty of eatables on the table which are lawful for a Jew to eat." "No," I exclaimed, "I cannot partake because I am a Christian;" and then taking out my Bible, I explained to him the utter uselessness of such charitable deeds when performed with the idea of securing the favour of God and the intercession of the saints. I told him at the same time, that remission of sins and entrance into heaven could only be procured through faith in Christ and entire dependence on His merits and atoning blood. The old man listened attentively, and appeared deeply moved. He again entreated me to have something to eat. I said, "I will do so, if the others stop eating until I have asked a blessing." He and the whole company agreed to this; and after offering prayer for about five minutes, I partook of some of the food, and as we departed, the host, with tears, bade me farewell, and asked me to pray for him and his family.

The next day we arrived in Kaselitz, after a six days' march from Kiev, and were lodged in the common prison of the town, where I had to remain two days. In the prison of Kaselitz I met with a Jewish family, who were imprisoned on account of the baptism of one of the children. The story was as follows:

A wealthy Russian fell in love with their daughter; they were attached to each other for a time without the knowledge of their parents. One day the girl, who was seventeen years of age, disappeared, and they heard after a few days that she had been baptized in the Russian Church. The family watched the house where she was said to be, hiding themselves a few days and nights until at last they succeeded in capturing her as she one evening was leaving the house. The girl could not refuse the tears and entreaties of her parents, and went home with them. Her lover soon became aware of this, and going to the police he bribed the officials to arrest the parents, which they did, and they were put into prison and the daughter restored to her lover.

From this, and from my own case, as before described, the reader will see that bribery will do a great deal in Russia. There is a proverb in the Russian language, which in English is as follows: "In Russia, everything is possible for money;" and the same is expressed in another Russian proverb: "God is high up, and the Czar is far off," which means the officials may do as they like if the money be forthcoming.

CHAPTER IX.

PRISONER CONDUCTED FROM KASELITZ TO TCHERNIGOV ; FIVE DAYS OF PROCLAIMING THE GOSPEL IN THE PRISON OF TCHERNIGOV ; ONE IMPRISONED FOR MORE THAN TWELVE YEARS WITHOUT TRIAL ; THE PRISON OF HOMEL, AND MY VISITORS ; MEETING WITH MY AGED MOTHER AND OTHER RELATIONS ; ARRIVAL IN MOHILEV, THE CAPITAL OF MY NATIVE PROVINCE ; EXTRACT FROM THE " FREE CHURCH RECORD.

DURING the two days of my imprisonment in Kaselitz, I had a very good opportunity of proclaiming the truth to both Jews and nominal Christians. The case of the imprisoned Jewish family, which I mentioned in the former chapter, supplied me with a good subject to show how both Russians and Jews are in darkness. The jailer used to come and sit for hours listening to me, and his presence commanded the silence of the prisoners, who also listened attentively to what I said. The jailer was sorry to part from me when I was compelled to continue my march, for he was very eager to hear the word of God.

After a march of four days on foot, and chained, as usual, with other prisoners, I arrived in Tchernigov, and was lodged with them in the common prison, where I remained for five days. There I met with a prisoner who had been twelve years in that prison without having been pronounced by a jury guilty of any crime. This was nothing new to me, as I had before seen prisoners incarcerated for two or three, and even more than five years, before they were committed for trial, though I had never before met with one who was imprisoned for the lengthened period of twelve years without having been committed for trial. The man was very intelligent, and I had many interesting conversations with him concerning the great salvation by faith in Christ; and I am thankful to say that I believe his soul was set free from sin, and saved by Jesus, through my feeble instrumentality. When I used to pray with him, he exclaimed: " Lord have mercy upon me, and forgive me all my transgressions." When I preached in the prison yard he used to gather the prisoners together, and kept them silent and attentive to what I spoke.

After a glorious mission-work of five days there, I was compelled to take another march on foot, and chained with a large number of prisoners. This march from Tchernigov to Homel lasted six days, marching from morning till night, notwithstanding the severity of the weather. Our meals consisted of brown bread of an inferior quality, and water to drink. Here and there the peasants had compassion on us, bringing us some warm soup. On the sixth day the weary journey was completed, and I arrived in Homel, and was lodged in the common prison, where I had to remain two days.

On the evening of my arrival in Homel I was visited by the relative who came as a deputy to Constantinople, and who was the author of my persecution. He at first spoke to me in a very friendly manner, and told me that I should be set at liberty at once if I only would give up my errors. I told him that my faith had not been weakened by the bitter sufferings I had undergone, but, on the contrary, strengthened; and that I considered it a privilege to suffer, and testify for my Lord and Master, who gave His life for me, that I might have everlasting life. My relative did not remain long to dispute with me, but came again next day, accompanied by several learned Jews, with whom I had a long discussion concerning the Messiah, whether He has already come or not. When I showed to them from Moses and the prophets that Jesus is the Messiah, and that they could only be saved by the free grace of God through Jesus, the only begotten Son of God, they departed with great anger from me.

Again, chained as formerly, I was obliged next day to undertake a march which lasted for two weeks, until I arrived in the capital of my native province of Mohilev. All the trials which I had hitherto endured, seemed as nothing in comparison to the journey from Homel to Mohilev. At a place where we had to remain for the night, I saw a large crowd advancing towards me, amongst whom I soon recognised many dear and familiar faces. My heart was wellnigh broken when I beheld my aged mother, my sisters, and their husbands and children, running towards me with cries and tears. I cannot tell you, dear reader, of the mental anguish of that moment, when my beloved mother, sinking in the dust before me, implored me, with heart-breaking sobs, to spare her the misery of going down to the grave with the knowledge that her best beloved son was an apostate and a traitor to his holy religion. It is too painful for me to describe further that scene. I have only reason to thank the Lord that He supported me in that trying moment when my mother was borne away fainting, and I was marched off to Mohilev, where I arrived on the 5th of January, 1870. There I was led off to the common prison, and next day I had the pleasure of a visit from the Protestant pastor—Rev. Mr. Bush—who took a deep interest in me, and exerted himself to the utmost to get me out of prison. My condition at that time has been described in a letter which appeared in the *Free Church Record* of April, 1870, from which I give the following extract:—

"In a more recent letter, Mr. Tomory gives a most affecting account of the present condition of the teacher Elieser, who, it will be recollected, was seized at Galata, and carried back to Russia:—

"'I have received a letter from Pastor Bush of Mohilev, and he tells me that Elieser arrived there on the 5th January. Exhausted by a ten weeks' march in a Russian winter, and under such circumstances, he got him into the prison hospital, where he will be cared for, for the moment, and be safe from the wrath and fury of the fanatical Jews. It seems that the poor man is entirely in their hands, and they intend to hand him over as a soldier for the Jewish community in the general conscription that is now taking place throughout Russia. Elieser is quite unfit for military service; but I suppose they will bribe the authorities, and with bribery you carry anything in that unhappy land. Mr. Bush tries to do what he can to avert such a fate from Elieser,—to be a menial or a camp-follower for fifteen to twenty years is certainly no joke,—but he was not sure that he would succeed.

"'We may soon hear again. Elieser is spiritually quite happy; his words are, "I will remain faithful to my Lord, and shall bear joyfully, with His assistance, all the persecution and opprobrium the enemy may be permitted to subject me to." The Lord indeed be his help and his protection! Mr. Bush says nothing of the governor-general, and I am afraid he is in the hands of the Jews.'"

CHAPTER X.

THE KINDNESS OF PASTOR BUSH, AND HIS ACTIVITY FOR MY LIBERATION; REMOVAL FROM PRISON DURING THE NIGHT, AND CONDUCTED TO BICHOV; THE WRATH OF THE JEWS, AND THE BURNING OF MY BIBLE; SECOND MEETING WITH MY MOTHER; THE JEWS RESOLVE TO PUT ME INTO THE RUSSIAN ARMY, BUT ARE UNSUCCESSFUL; REMOVAL FROM BICHOV AND MEETING WITH A RUSSIAN PRIEST, TO WHOM I ADDRESSED MYSELF FOR HELP, AND THE CONSEQUENCE OF IT.

IN the foregoing chapter the reader will have observed how the kind Protestant pastor got me into the prison hospital, not only because he saw my exhausted state, but also that I might be free from the wrath and fury of the fanatical Jews. He was also very active in trying to procure my liberation; and it seemed to us both that I should soon be set free.

On one of his visits the good pastor informed me of this, when I heartily thanked God that at length my sufferings were about to terminate; but although man proposes, it is God that disposes. I afterwards found that but one act of the drama had as yet been enacted, and a new scene of persecution was about to set in, much more difficult to bear than the first.

One evening in January I was called out of my cell in the hospital, to the offices of the prison, where

I found my clothes lying in a bundle, and I was ordered by the jailer to dress. I thought the time of my liberation had come, and gladly dressed myself, though my clothes did look very shabby, having passed through thirteen prisons from Constantinople to Mohilev. As soon as I was dressed, two soldiers came in and asked me to follow them. I was conducted to the door of the office, where a sleigh with two gendarmes awaited me. I was invited to take a seat between them, and the driver was ordered to drive as speedily as he could. We travelled all night, and early in the morning we found ourselves in Bichov, a town in the government of Mohilev, about fifty miles from the capital of the province. I must not omit to mention that at the beginning of our journey, and when only a short way out of the city, a large number of Jews awaited me, who, when they saw the sleigh in which I was, took their seats in sleighs which were waiting for them, and drove after us.

About twenty-five miles from Mohilev, we halted at an inn to rest the horses. The Jews came to me where I was in a room with the gendarmes, and said: "Now we have got you away from Mohilev, where your friend the Protestant pastor expects to-morrow that you shall be free, and that he shall gain the victory over us; but he shall not even know where you are, and we shall do with you as we please." My heart was so full that I remained silent. I only lifted my heart to the Lord, and prayed that He might deliver me from their cruel hands, and might open their eyes to see their injustice towards me.

When we arrived in Bichov, the gendarmes conveyed me to the police office, and the chief of the police, who had been richly bribed by the Jews, delivered me into their hands to do with me as they liked. I demanded of him whether it was not his duty rather to protect a Christian from the wrath of the Jews, but gold was more precious to him than Christ.

The Jews took me away from the police office and brought me into a Jewish house, where a room was prepared for me, and four Jews appointed to watch me. Day by day, from morning till evening the most learned of the Jews came to dispute with me; and although I knew that my life was in danger, I was not afraid to speak of the truth which is in Christ Jesus.

One day, as I disputed with a large number of Jews, and after some hours of earnest conversation, the audience were divided concerning me; one half demanded my liberation, but the other said that it was a command of their rabbis to destroy an apostate, and that whoever killed such, had done a good deed. Between these two contending parties I was nearly torn in pieces. My enemies became so bitter that they snatched from me my New Testament, which I had in Hebrew, and a Bible in German, which Pastor Bush brought to me in the prison of Mohilev, and flung them both into the fire. When I exclaimed that by destroying the books they could not deprive me of the portions which were written on my memory, "Be silent, apostate, or we will burn thee also," was the fierce retort. My mother, who was present, begged of me to be silent, or they would kill me. I replied, "Dear mother, you know how I ever dearly loved you, and it is not lack of love which prevents me from now doing your will, but it is the Spirit of God which compels me to speak, and as for being afraid that the Jews will kill me, I say that they could not do me a greater kindness, for I would thus be released from my sufferings, and at once be in the presence of my beloved Saviour, whom I long to behold." My dear mother left me and returned home, because she could neither witness my cruel treatment, nor yet hear me speak of Christ and His grace.

Some of the Jews seemed to be touched by what I said, but the majority, enraged beyond all bounds, would have beaten me to death, had not the others interposed to rescue me. With great difficulty the more peaceably inclined Jews induced their companions to leave me alone, at least. At length they all returned to their homes, and I was left in care of the four Jews, who kept watch by me.

The resolution of my enemies was to bribe the officials, in order to take me into the Russian army. They imagined that the idea of serving fifteen years in the army would be sufficient to make me return to the Jewish faith. They bribed all the officials, and it seemed as if they would be able to carry out their plot at once, as I was taken to the military office. But to the great surprise of every one, an order came from the chief office of the provinces declaring me free, and saying that the military office should not by any means accept me for the army.

I was extremely glad to find justice at last. I left the office and determined to go at once to Mohilev. But my joy was of short duration, for scarcely had I left the office when I was caught by several Jews and dragged into a house where many Jews were assembled. They were all filled with bitter hate against me, and bound themselves to destroy me, ere any of my Christian friends could come to my rescue. They bribed both police and magistrates heavily to wink at their proceedings, and their resolution was to take me to another place where none of my friends would hear of me; so that they might do with me what they pleased. But some of their number, more friendly disposed towards me, and fearing some dire catastrophe would befall me, refused to allow me to be removed. A quarrel ensued. My enemies proved strongest. Some caught me by the arms, others by the legs, and others by the hair, while the rest struck me in the face until it was covered with blood. In this condition they brought me out of the house, and pitched me into a sledge, which stood at the door waiting for my reception. Three of these Jews took their seats in the sledge with me, and the driver was told to drive as speedily as possible. Many of the others accompanied us in other sledges. We travelled the whole night, and at daybreak the procession halted at an inn, on the highway, for the purpose of offering their morning prayers. During the time they offered their prayers I was left in a room, where warm water was brought to wash the blood off my face. Meanwhile a Russian priest entered the apartment where I was alone. My pallid countenance and cast-down expression touched the priest's heart with pity, and after a few questions he had an idea of my sufferings. Burning with indignation, he started from his seat, saying that there was a Government official in the adjoining chamber, that he would go and lay my case before him, and I should at once obtain redress. My tormentors soon became aware of what was transpiring, and they were summoned before the officer, but they contrived to make out so plausible a tale that both the judge and the priest repented having so warmly espoused my cause, and I did not see the face of the priest again. The Jews now came with wrath and bitter hate to the apartment where I was waiting, expecting to be released through the exertions of the priest, and having administered many blows until my face was again covered with blood, they put me in the before-mentioned sledge, and, after a few hours' driving, we arrived at Luravitz, which is entirely a Jewish town.

CHAPTER XI.

HEAVY FETTERS, AND MY FEELINGS WHEN I WAS BOUND IN THEM; ADDRESS TO JEWISH WOMEN, AND THE CONSEQUENCE OF IT; A HAPPY DAY OF PROCLAIMING THE GOSPEL TO MANY JEWS IN THE INN, AND IN THE HOUSE OF THE RABBI; REMOVAL FROM LURAVITZ TO AN INN ON THE HIGHWAY, WHERE A CONFERENCE WAS HELD; THE JEWS DIVIDED; ONE PARTY ABOUT TO DROWN ME IN THE RIVER DNIEPER, WHEN THE OTHERS CAME TO MY RESCUE.

IT was Friday when our procession reached Luravitz, and I was placed in a Jewish house, where a watch of four men was set to guard me. I was not long in the house when there entered several Jews bearing heavy chains. It was a painful sight to me, and I suddenly appeared to be endowed with supernatural strength, as a voice seemed to whisper, "Wrest those irons from the hands of the bloodhounds who are thirsting to drain to the very last drop thy heart's-blood, and, by a few well-aimed blows, stretch them lifeless on the ground. Thou art perfectly justified in acting thus in self-defence." The temptation was overwhelming. My hand was raised to seize the fetters, but a flash of light crossed my mind with the remembrance of the words of our Lord to Peter: "Put up thy sword again into his place, for all they that take the sword shall perish with the sword." I then cried out, "O my Father! not my will, but Thine be done." My hand dropped, and without resistance I suffered myself to be again bound in fetters.

The peace which pervaded my soul since my persecution became now turned into joy, and I kneeled down in the presence of the large assemblage of Jews—men, women, and children—and returned thanks audibly to my blessed Saviour, who had counted me worthy to suffer for His holy name's sake, and had been present with me amid all my conflicts and trials. When I rose from my knees I found the room empty, save for the Jews who were left to watch me.

In the evening, which was the eve of the Jewish Sabbath, many women came to see me, amongst whom were the wives of several of the most influential Jewish residents. After some conversation, I proposed that they should join with me in a short service, to which they immediately agreed; and after I sang a psalm, and offered prayer, I gave them a short address. The women wept bitterly as I explained to them the reason why they are a scattered people among all the nations —viz., because they have not accepted the Messiah, who came not only to give them happiness in this world, but, greater than this, to give happiness which would last through the ages of eternity. I could see that my words made a deep impression on them, and at parting they promised to use their utmost influence with their husbands to procure my release. That they kept their promise I saw from what occurred next day.

Early next morning, a smith came and relieved me of the heavy fetters with which I was bound, and so a certain amount of freedom was given me. The whole day, the saloon of the house where I was lodged was crowded with Jews, who came to see me; and I preached salvation by Christ from morning till evening. I was very happy that day to have the privilege of proclaiming the glorious Gospel to so many of my brethren. Later in the evening, I was invited by the rabbi to his house, where many Jews were assembled. My host asked me to sit by his side, and explain to him my doctrine concerning the Messiah. I then quoted passage after passage from the Old Testament, and explained to them the necessity of a Saviour and the time of His coming, and that all the prophecies which exist concerning the Messiah cannot be applied to any one except to Jesus, whom they despised. The rabbi and some of the Jews were touched by my arguments, but most of them were enraged, and became so angry that they even regretted having granted me the favour of releasing me from my chains. I was forcibly dragged away from the rabbi's house, and with kicks and blows brought back to the inn, where I was placed under a strong guard of Jews.

Next day I was taken from that place to an inn not far from the banks of the river Dnieper. That place was chosen for a place of conference, as it lay between several towns, and was thus suitable for that purpose. The rabbis and many Jews from each town came, and I was asked to tell again my doctrine concerning the Messiah. This time I brought my arguments concerning the Messiah, and the time of His coming, not only from Moses and the Prophets, but also from the rabbinical books. These arguments, which they could not controvert, cut them to the heart. With a loud cry of mingled rage and hatred, many of them rushed upon me and shouted, "What? apostate! dog! thou darest still to speak of the Crucified! Now shalt thou live no longer! We will drown thee in the Dnieper like a miserable dog! According to our rabbinical law, it is a command of God to destroy the apostates."

No sooner said than done. They laid hold of me and pulled me, some by my beard, another by my hair; some by the arms, and others by the feet; and flung me into a sledge, all the time bestowing on me a plentiful shower of blows which caused the blood to flow, and inflicted wounds, the scars of which are still to be seen. I felt at that time that the hour of my departure from this world had arrived, and I commended my soul into the hands of the Lord.

We soon reached the river, and some of them hastened to cut a hole in the thick ice, while others dragged me from the sledge. When the hole was cut, they carried me to the opening, and were about to push me in, when the noise of a great crowd was heard rapidly approaching. They pushed me in with great difficulty, the hole being too narrow, and so the skin of my legs and body was greatly grazed. When they had succeeded with the lower parts of my body, they found that my arms would not allow the upper parts of my body to pass through, and so were about to break them, when the Jews who were friendly disposed to me arrived in time to save me. There was a shout as of two contending armies rushing to battle. One group, bent on rescuing me, dragged me out of the water; the other seized me and wanted to force me back, and so between friends and foes I fared worse than with foes alone. The scene baffles all description; the details are too harrowing for me to dwell upon, and also for the reader. It is sufficient to say that my rescuers succeeded in pulling me out of the water, and carried me in an insensible condition to the inn, where I was restored to consciousness. The next day a stream of my foes came, accompanied by an overwhelming number of inimical Jews, and hurried me away to Bichov.

CHAPTER XII.

MY CASE TAKEN UP BY JEWS OF ALL PARTS OF THE PROVINCE; ADDRESSING A LARGE ASSEMBLY OF JEWS WHO WERE THEN DIVIDED IN THEIR OPINIONS TOWARDS ME; A GENERAL COUNCIL HELD, AND RESOLUTION TO PUT ME INTO THE RUSSIAN ARMY; THE JEWS BRIBE THE VICE-GOVERNOR, AND I AM ACCEPTED IN THE ARMY; MY STRUGGLE WITH THE OFFICERS CONCERNING THE OATH; START FOR HEADQUARTERS.

ON our arrival in Bichov, I was placed in an inn under a strong guard of Jews. The friendly disposed came also to that town, and brought with them Jews from different towns. My case was now taken up by Jews from all parts of the province. I was brought before the chief rabbi, and, in the presence of a large assembly, was requested to state how it was that I, a pious orthodox Jew, had been induced to renounce Judaism and embrace Christianity? I talked to them for three hours, proving how the Messiah had already come, and that Jesus is the Messiah. When I ceased a regular tumult ensued, and the assembly was divided into two parties—one crying: "He is an apostate, and according to the law of our rabbis (blessed be their memory!) he must be destroyed;" the other demanding space for the consideration of the measures to be adopted. At length it was settled that a general council should take place, and meanwhile I should be placed under strict surveillance.

At this council a resolution was passed to set me free; but as the members were preparing to leave, a very rich Jew, who had been silent the whole time, burst forth indignantly : " What ! an apostate whom we have in our hands, and can do with him what we like, to allow him to go free? According to our laws he ought to be stoned." Immediately there was a division, and, after a long debate, it was agreed to use all means in order to make me enter the army. A deputation was appointed to Mohilev to bribe the Government officials, which they easily did in all the courts but one, where the president was a Protestant, and also a friend to Pastor Bush, and to whom the good clergyman told everything about me. The Jews now seeing it impossible to bribe that court, they tried and succeeded in bribing the vice-governor of the province; and, as the governor-general was absent at that time, the vice-governor, being in power, gave an order to the Military Conscription Court to accept me for the army. On the 12th of February, 1870, the order of the vice-governor was received in Bichov, in spite of the protestations of the president of the supreme court of the province, to the effect that I was free from military duties.

When I was brought into the Military Conscription Court, where several officials were sitting, and they told me to take the oath of allegiance, I exclaimed firmly : " Is it possible that you require of me to take the oath, though you are fully aware of the injustice you do to me—knowing, as you do, that the law frees me from military duties? Besides, you see that I am so weak as to be totally unfit for the service, but for the sake of a little Jewish gold you are base enough to accept me! Look at my still unhealed wounds, and say truly whether you are not guilty of perjury of the deepest dye? O ye hypocrites! how will ye be able to stand before the righteous Judge?"

The officers were silent. The chief of them retired into an adjoining room, where many Jews were assembled, and after a long conversation with them he returned. He glanced compassionately at me, and said, "Dear brother! do not distress yourself. We know well that you are not only free but totally unfit for military duties; but we are not to blame for your summons to the army, as we received an order from the Government to receive you immediately into military service, and that order we must obey. However, you will not have to remain longer than eight days in the army, as the Jews must find a substitute for you." I was too well acquainted with the system of bribery in Russia to believe this plausible tale, but all my representations failing, I saw too plainly that I should have to submit to the force of circumstances, and join the army, though I hated to do so.

But now a new difficulty arose. The Jews insisted that the oath should be administered to me in their synagogue, intending by this ruse to make it appear that I had denied my Saviour, and renounced Christianity. The officer endeavoured to induce me to do so, but on this point I was immovable. In burning language I reproved the officers for aiding and abetting my persecutors, and bringing discredit on the holy name of Christ. Somewhat abashed, they at length agreed to send me to Mohilev, to take the oath there, in the Protestant place of worship, as there was none in Bichov. But the Jews being afraid that, if I went to Mohilev, where my friend, Pastor Bush resided, I should be released, again resorted to bribing the officers, and arrangements were made that the oath should be administered to me in the Greek Church. When I was brought before the priest there, I said to him : " I am a Protestant, and therefore I shall neither make the sign of the cross nor yet kiss the golden cross, which you hold in your hand during the administration of the oath." The priest agreed, and administered the oath to me and to a Russian who had to take it at that time. The officer who was appointed to witness, was not satisfied that I did not conform to the usual mode, and when we left the church he entered into hot discourse with me, and in his anger was ready to use the strongest military discipline upon me; but I used the " sword of the Spirit," and he appeared softened. He left me in charge of a soldier, and went hastily away.

A few days afterwards, in company with a body of raw recruits, I was ordered to start for headquarters, to be drilled for six months, and prepared for active service. Our march lasted a week, and on the seventh day we arrived at Homel, the headquarters for recruits.

CHAPTER XIII.

DESCRIPTION OF BARRACKS IN GOMEL; HOW I WAS APPRECIATED BY MY SUPERIORS AND FELLOW-SOLDIERS; VISITED BY MY MOTHER AND OTHER RELATIVES; MY PECULIAR KIND OF PREACHING TO THE JEWS IN GOMEL; EXPECTING DAILY TO BE RELEASED FROM THE ARMY; EXTRACT FROM THE "FREE CHURCH RECORD;" TRANSFERRED TO THE 24TH REGIMENT OF INFANTRY; ATTEND THE FULL CURRICULUM OF THE MILITARY MEDICAL COLLEGE; APPOINTED AS MEDICAL OFFICER IN THE MILITARY HOSPITAL; MY MISSION WORK IN WARSAW; MY MILITARY UNIFORM AFFORDING PROTECTION FROM THE WRATH OF THE JEWS, WHEN I SPOKE TO THEM OF JESUS.

ON my arrival in Gomel with my companions, I was placed in the barracks with 1000 recruits, with whom I was daily drilled in the use of arms and war signals. These recruits were divided into four companies of 250 each, who occupied one very large room. In the middle of the room stood a long, broad, wooden bench, which reached from one end to the other. On both sides of it were mattresses filled with straw on which the men slept head to head. In the morning the mattresses were folded away, and the half of the bench served as a table, at which the meals were taken. At noon we had soup made with sour cabbage, which was not very palatable; five times a-week the soup was cooked with meat, besides the cabbage, and each got a small piece of it. I am not sure that we got the tenth part of a pound! Towards evening the meal consisted of a very thin soup without meat, or even fat. The bread was black, and of bad quality.

On the day after my arrival I, with another recruit, was ordered to carry water to the kitchen. This work I found rather heavy, as I was very weak. I prayed to the Lord for help, and He soon answered my prayer, for the next day the sergeant, noticing my abilities, introduced me to the sergeant-major, and then to the captain of the company. I was appointed at once as an elder of ten recruits, and after some days I was chosen by the whole company as leader of the company's committee. Soon after this appointment I found a way by which the food might be improved, and my plan succeeded so well that I was asked by the captains of the other companies to introduce my method into their companies. The Lord was with me in everything I had to do, and I felt that I was beloved by my superiors as well as by my inferiors.

I was not long in Gomel when my mother and some relatives came to see me, and they remained in that town for a few weeks, in order to persuade me to renounce Christianity and return to the Jewish faith. This was a trying time for me; the daily scenes I had with my relations are too painful to describe.

During the time I was in Gomel, I daily visited the Jews in their houses and synagogues, and preached to them the gospel of salvation. Many hundred Jews used to come to see how the "apostate young rabbi" was drilled; and after drill, I had the permission of my superiors to speak to them. Although often tired, I never lost an opportunity of pointing the way of salvation to my Jewish brethren. I used to preach for a couple of hours in the open air, gun in hand, and they were all very attentive to hear. My Christian friends at this time were not idle; they used every means to procure my release; but nothing could be accomplished until the time appointed by the Lord, as the reader may see from an extract of the *Free Church Record* of September, 1870 :—

"*Rev. A. Tomory to F. Brown-Douglas, Esq.*

"Elieser is still a soldier. The command for his liberation has come down from St. Petersburg long ago; but the Jews bribed the local authorities, and they hinder it. I had to write again to St. Petersburg, and I trust that by this time another peremptory order has come down from St. Petersburg, and the poor prisoner may soon be free. Meanwhile, the Lord works mightily by him. Numbers of Jews, who never heard the free Gospel message, are now listening daily to Elieser. As a soldier he is quite free to speak what he likes,—his letters are thrilling. Were there space for them in the *Record*, I could translate some of them. His soul is prospering under the heavy afflictions, and in the midst of troubles and sorrows of all kinds his soul is full of joy. In his last letter he says : 'My sorrows are great, but my joys are still greater when I am enabled to speak to so many Jews in the heart of Russia about the Lord Jesus.' He asks us to send Hebrew New Testaments and tracts for the Jews. But alas! Russia does not permit such articles to pass its frontiers. We will still try."

Several months passed in which I expected day by day to be released from the Russian army, but the Jewish bribery prolonged it; and at the end of the summer of 1870, when the drilling battalion was dissolved, and the young soldiers were appointed to active service in different regiments, I was appointed to the 24th Regiment of Infantry, whose headquarters were in Russian Poland.

The day after my arrival in that regiment, I was chosen as clerk of the company; and when I had been a fortnight in that position, I was taken as clerk to the office of the regiment. I was not there long until I was sent as student to the Military Medical College, where I attended the full curriculum of three years, and passed my examination. I was then appointed as medical officer to the Military Hospital in Warsaw.

During my four years' stay in Warsaw, I had a good opportunity of serving the King of Kings. My daily prayers were as follow: In the morning I prayed, "Lord Jesus, Thou hast done so much for me, what can I do for Thee to-day? My Saviour, my Lord and Master! what wilt Thou have me to do in Thy field to-day?" In the evening I used to inquire of myself what I had that day done for my Saviour, who had done so much for me; and if I found that I had had an opportunity of doing something for Christ, I returned thanks that He, the King of Kings, had counted me worthy of His service. If I found that I had done nothing that day for the promotion of the Kingdom of Christ on earth, I prayed, "Lord, make me worthy of Thy service, I am ready to serve Thee; guide me to the work which Thou wouldest have me to do."

I assure you, dear reader, no one will be more happy than when engaged in the business of his heavenly Father; only then can we fully realise that we have a loving Father, who lives and reigns for ever. And, according to my humble experience, I may say that every one, in whatever capacity the Lord has placed him, is able to be about the business of his Father. I will try, for the encouragement of some fellow-Christian, to give some instances of how I was enabled at that time to be about the business of my heavenly Father.

When I was placed in the Military Medical College in Warsaw, I had much class work to do besides my work in the hospital. I never forgot, however, that my call from the Lord is to preach the Gospel to my Jewish brethren. For that purpose I used to go day by day to visit the Jews in their houses, synagogues, coffee-houses, restaurants, and in their places of business, where I proclaimed to them the way of salvation.

On one Saturday afternoon I went to a synagogue and preached there to a large assembly of Jews for some hours. They listened very attentively as long as I spoke to them of repentance, and the necessity of atonement; but when I told them that we only can be saved by the free grace and the atoning blood of Jesus Christ, who is the angel of whom Job speaks in chap. xxxiii. 23, 24 ("If there be a messenger with him, an interpreter, one among a thousand, to show unto man his uprightness; then he is gracious unto him, and saith, Deliver him from going down to the pit; I have found a ransom "), they became noisy, and were ready to strike me, and to cast me out of the synagogue. When I saw this, I said calmly: "Keep your temper, and behold whom you have before you. Think of the consequences if you lay a finger upon me; for although I would pardon you, and say, 'Father, forgive them; for they know not what they do,' yet Alexander II., whose uniform I wear, would not pardon you for offending one who is in his service; for the assault would not only be to me, but to him; therefore, take my advice and calm yourselves." They at once became silent, and the ruler of the synagogue asked me in a very respectful manner to leave the synagogue, and not disturb them in their prayers which they were about to offer. Before I left, I read to them part of the 18th and the 33rd chapters of Ezekiel. As I passed out, I took some of the water which stood at the door for the purpose of washing the hands before prayers, and washing mine, I said, addressing myself to the assembly, "See, I wash my hands as a token to you that I am clean of your blood. I have done my duty according to the Word of God, as I have just read to you from the Prophet Ezekiel." With these words I left the synagogue.

On another occasion, I went in company with Mr. Ifland, a missionary, to a café, where many Jews were discussing various topics. The missionary entered into conversation with some of the bystanders, while I proceeded into an inner room and joined a group of Jews, and was soon engaged with them in earnest arguments. The controversy, though it waxed warm, was conducted with perfect good temper, but loud voices and sounds as of a scuffle were heard from the apartment where Mr. Ifland was. I hastened in and found my friend surrounded with Jews, who seemed all in a perfect uproar. I seated myself beside him, and the sight of my military uniform worked wonders. Order was at once restored, and the conversation was carried on in an animated but not in an angry strain. One of their number said to me: "We like to hear, when you speak, because we know it is not for money you do so; but the missionary only speaks for money, and, therefore, we despise him. "But, dear friend," said I, "the question is not whether he speaks for money or not, but whether his words be true. You do not despise Mr. Filtzer, the owner of the café, for selling his coffee, cakes, &c.; but you taste and see, then if they are good you come again and, perhaps, bring a friend, by saying, 'If you wish to have good coffee or cake come to Mr. Filtzer.' Why not do the same with Mr. Ifland? Taste and try if you like the sweet words which he presents to you. You do not pay for them as you do to Mr. Filtzer for his goods; and if you like them ask for more, and bring a friend that he may also partake." These words seemed to calm the audience, and they listened to the Gospel message.

In my daily hospital work I used to speak to the sick of their spiritual diseases, and then pray with them. Among my fellow-students I became a by-word. "Bassin is curing the sick in the hospital with prayer," was their cry; but this did not discourage me in the least.

CHAPTER XIV.

MY FIRST JOURNEY FROM WARSAW TO MY NATIVE PLACE; A CONDITIONAL INVITATION FROM A COUSIN OF MINE; WHAT BECAME OF THE MONEY SENT FROM SCOTLAND TO BUY ME OUT OF THE ARMY; SECOND JOURNEY TO MY NATIVE PLACE; THE ILLNESS OF MY MOTHER; MY EARNEST CONVERSATION WITH HER, AND THE CONSEQUENCE OF IT; MY RETURN TO WARSAW AND TRANSFER TO ST. PETERSBURG; MY EXCHANGING WORDS WITH THE EMPEROR ALEXANDER II.

DURING my sojourn in Warsaw, I made two journeys to my native place. The first was in 1871, and my object in going was to buy myself off from the army; for, as the reader may have observed in the preceding chapter, all the efforts which my Christian friends had made for my liberation had been thus far frustrated by the bribery of the Jews. My Christian friends in Scotland, knowing this, sympathised with me, and sent £70 in order that I should buy myself off, as it was a rule in Russia at that time that one can be free by paying a certain sum of money. I therefore went to Mohilev, as the money would be accepted only there; but the Lord's time had not yet come, for even this generous effort proved of no avail, because I had been illegally placed in the army, and therefore the money could not be legally accepted. My journey, however, was not in vain, for I had once more the opportunity of preaching the good tidings of salvation in the places where I had been persecuted. From morning till night I was visited by Jews, to whom I preached the Gospel. I visited them here also in their houses, synagogues, and places of business, and was cordially received on the whole.

To the house of a cousin I was invited, on condition that I should not speak of Christ. I agreed on condition that they should not speak against Christ, for I very well knew that they would not be able to speak with me without doing so. When I came to his house many of my relations were already assembled, and they very soon commenced to speak against the Christian religion; and as soon as they did so, I was at liberty to speak of Christ and his salvation. So long as I dwelt on man's fallen and sinful nature, and on the necessity of atonement by the shedding of blood, all listened quietly; but when I proceeded to point out how, by the sacrifice of Christ, once offered on Calvary, one only and all-sufficient atonement had been made, a regular uproar ensued, and the men, women, and even the children cried, "Beat him! beat him!" But my cousin who had invited me to his house interfered, saying that I had kept my word in not speaking of Christ as long as they did not abuse Him. My cousin's words calmed the audience, who soon after quietly dispersed to their homes, and I returned to my hotel. Next day I went back to Warsaw, to continue my studies in the Medical College.

The £70 which was sent from Scotland to buy me

out of the army was now converted by the Free Church Jewish Mission Committee as a help in pursuing my studies, for which I was very thankful, and I cannot now omit this opportunity of giving to them my hearty thanks once more.

My second journey to Mohilev was in 1874, when I got a telegram from my mother, informing me of her illness, and saying that she wished to see me before she died. On receiving these sad tidings, I hurried to the Military Office, and getting leave of absence, I hastened to the place of my childhood. On my arrival I went to my mother's sick room, where I found my two sisters. My parent, though very ill, was in possession of all her faculties, and as soon as I entered the room, and stood beside her bed, and we had kissed each other, she asked my sisters to leave the room, and in a low voice she commenced to speak to me as follows:—

"My dear son, I have carefully watched over you from your infancy, and I had the hope that, through your piety and prayers, I shall be delivered from the punishment of hell; for although I have done nothing wrong in this world—you know what a pious woman I have been, you know of my good works—yet a purgatorial process is necessary, as you know, according to the doctrine of our rabbis (blessed be their memory!); even the righteous of the earth are subject to a certain punishment in hell. In order that they should be cleansed from their stains, and be delivered from this purgatorial punishment, there is only one remedy, and that is the daily prayers and piety of good sons."

My heart was wellnigh broken to see my beloved

mother, at the end of her life, after hearing so much as she had done about Christ, still strong in her belief that good works and prayers offered by sons after death, could be of any avail.

"My dear mother," I exclaimed, with tears in my eyes, "prayer for the dead did not originate with the Jews. You will not find the practice of praying for the dead anywhere in the Bible; the Jews brought it with them after the Babylonian captivity, and only from the time of the Maccabees was this doctrine put in writing, as it is stated in 2nd Maccabees, chap. xii. But, dear mother, the true Scriptural doctrine is that we can be saved only by the free grace of God, and the blood of Christ now cleanseth us from all our sins, as did the blood of the sacrifices, in the old dispensation."

My mother became angry, and said: "Speak not to me of the Crucified One. I believe only in the true God; leave the room and even the house at once. I cannot think of being under the roof with an apostate, and he one of my own children."

With tears, I left the apartment, and could only pray that, ere it was too late, her eyes might be enlightened, and she might be permitted to acknowledge Jesus as her Saviour. I left my mother's house immediately, but remained in Mohilev for a few weeks, until my leave of absence expired, and I was compelled to return to my post at Warsaw.

On my arrival there a change awaited me. I was ordered as manager of apothecary in the Military Hospital of the First Body-guard of Artillery in St. Petersburg, and at the end of the summer of 1874,

I entered on my new office in St. Petersburg. I was not long there, till I was advanced to a higher office, with a better salary, and appointed manager of apothecary in the Hospital of the Military College of the Russian nobility. There I once had an opportunity of exchanging a few words with the Emperor Alexander II., when he asked me, "How many people have you sent to heaven?" My reply was, "Not more than heaven requested of me."

CHAPTER XV.

THE FIRST-FRUIT OF MY WORK IN ST. PETERSBURG; THE BAPTISM OF MR. KUKURIZKIN, A JEW OF THE SECT OF THE KARAITES; MY HAPPINESS IN BEING ABOUT THE BUSINESS OF MY HEAVENLY FATHER; CIRCLE OF CHRISTIAN FRIENDS IN ST. PETERSBURG, AND BIBLE-CLASSES AT COUNT KORFF'S; THE SECRETARY OF THE LONDON JEWISH MISSIONARY SOCIETY IN ST. PETERSBURG, AND MY COMING IN CONTACT WITH THAT SOCIETY; LETTERS FROM REV. A. TOMORY CONCERNING THE FREE CHURCH OF SCOTLAND AND THE EPISCOPAL CHURCH; MY STUDIES IN THEOLOGY.

IN the foregoing chapter the reader has seen how the Lord was with me in prospering the work of my hands in my military office, and in this chapter I will endeavour to give some account of the grace of God,—how He, the King of Kings, accounted me worthy to do some work for His kingdom.

The first opportunity I had was on the next day after my arrival, when I visited Pastor Dalton, who had taken a deep interest in me during my persecution and imprisonment, &c. He told me that an Israelite of the Karaite sect had applied to him for baptism, but the young man did not know German, and he himself did not know sufficient Russian or Hebrew to instruct him in the Christian religion. Pastor Dalton further said that he had asked Pastor

Mazing, who was well acquainted with the Russian language, to instruct him; but he would prefer if I could render him this service, because I knew best how to deal with Jews. I willingly consented to this, and on the same day visited Pastor Mazing. Next day Mr. Kukurizkin was sent to me with an introduction from Pastor Mazing. I found that young man a thorough gentleman and highly educated. I instructed him for several weeks in the doctrines of Christianity, and I felt that the spirit of the Lord was working daily more and more in his soul. Very often, when we prayed together, tears filled his eyes. The weeks during which he was instructed was a time of delight to my soul, and when I found I could say in regard to his case, as the Apostle of old said, "Can any man forbid water that these should not be baptised which have received the Holy Ghost as well as we?" I brought him to Pastor Dalton, who examined him, and administered to him the rite of baptism.

I visited the Jews nearly every day, in their houses, synagogues, and places of business, where I proclaimed the Word of God. I was also visited daily by Jews, and felt happy each day in being about the business of my heavenly Father. My circle of Christian friends grew day by day, and very often I was led to say with the Psalmist, "Behold how good and how pleasant a thing it is for brethren to dwell together in unity."

Through my intimate and honourable friends, Count Zaremba and Count Korff, I was invited to the houses of the highest nobility of Russia; and soon the Lord gave me the privilege of holding a Bible class for the Russian aristocracy. This class was held in an unusual way. On the Tuesday Count Korff invited his noble friends, to whom I used to explain the Bible from the original. I commenced at eight o'clock and spoke till ten, during which time each of the listeners took notes, and from ten till twelve questions were put to me, which I answered. At midnight the meeting was over, but usually many remained, and we had a free conversation concerning the truth of the Word of God till two o'clock in the morning. These six hours passed so quickly that they seemed to me as only one hour.

Count Korff used to take me also to the houses of his friends and acquaintances; and I was happy, and heartily thanked the Lord for accounting me worthy of His service, and allowing me to do a good work for the Greek Church. For I must not omit to mention that Count Korff, as well as all who attended my Bible class, were members of the Greek Church.

In the beginning of 1875, the Secretary of the London Society for Promoting Christianity amongst the Jews, the Rev. F. Smith, came to St. Petersburg with a petition from his Society, asking the Emperor for permission to work amongst the Jews in Russia. The permission was granted; and the secretary, taking a warm interest in me and in my voluntary mission work, I thus came in contact with the London Jewish Mission Society. A call was given to me to leave my medical office in the army, and to enter into the service of that society. Although I was glad to enter on such a noble profession as missionary, yet I was sorry not to be able to work in connection with the Church and Mission through whose instrumentality I was brought to Christ, and from which I received great sympathy. I therefore wrote to Rev. A. Tomory, asking his fatherly advice, and received from him the following answer (original in German):—

"GALATA, 20th *January*, 1875.

"MY DEAR ELIESER,—The Lord bless you in the new year, and renew His grace to you to serve Him in true righteousness and holiness! Erect a new Ebenezer, and say, 'Hitherto hath the Lord helped me.' May He help you also farther! We often think of you, and pray for you. We are very glad to hear what you say about the permission for the Jewish Mission in Poland and Russia. May the Lord open many doors and many hearts! I shall be very glad if you join the English Mission there. The Lord give you His blessing! It is one Church, and we have no mission there. You will let us know what answer you get from the English Mission, and the name of the missionary who will come to St. Petersburg from the Episcopal Church. The Lord grant that thousands of Jews shall hear the word of salvation, and shall become believers!

"We rejoice to hear that your Karaite was baptised. The Lord give him His free grace, that he may live a faithful life! Marko, our assistant teacher, is not yet baptised; but he is an earnest believer. My wife and children, and all friends, send their regards to you.—With warm love, yours,

"ALEXANDER TOMORY."

As soon as I received this advice from Mr. Tomory, I offered myself as a labourer in the mission field, in connection with the London Society for Promoting Christianity among the Jews; and having answered a number of printed questions which it is usual for the Society to submit to their candidates, they determined to take me into their service, as soon as I should obtain my discharge from the army.

In the meantime, I received another letter from

Mr. Tomory, saying that there was hope that the Free Church of Scotland would also have a mission to the Jews in Russia; and that he (Mr. Tomory) should rejoice if I could remain in the Church where I had received the Gospel, and which had assisted me with love and money during the time of my need. I was very happy to hear this, and I waited for some months for a decision from the Free Church Jewish Mission Committee. At length I had the following letter from Rev. A. Tomory:—

"GALATA, 15th *November*, 1875.

"MY DEAR ELIESER,—To-day I have received a letter from the Committee, and they do not know *how, where*, or *when* they will have a mission in Russia; therefore they have not decided anything. Wait no longer, but accept the offer of the London Jewish Mission Society, without further loss of time. I should very much like to see you in the service of our Church, partly because you would serve us, but much more because the Episcopalians are strangers to you; but we must see the hand of God directing such things, and submit to it. Man proposes, but God disposes." . . .

Accordingly I accepted the resolution of the London Jewish Mission Committee, to work in conjunction with their missionary, Rev. D. A. Hefter, who came to St. Petersburg to open the mission there. But we were soon informed that no mission work should be done in St. Petersburg, or in any other place in Russia, until the committee of the senators, which were appointed to consider the matter of the mission, knew how far the permission of the Czar was intended. Until that time, the missionaries were advised by the Prime Minister not to remain in Russia. The London Society therefore resolved that Mr. Hefter should return to his station at Frankfort-on-the-Main, and that I should go for a time to Germany, on their account, and prepare myself for my future mission work. After that, they resolved that I should be trained in their Missionary College in London. Accordingly I went there, 5th October, 1876. My training under the auspices of the London Jewish Mission Society was first for about ten months in Germany, and then fifteen months in London.

The discipline in the College, in which the students also resided, was rather too strict; for although I had been accustomed to a rigid discipline in the Russian army, I certainly found it objectionable in the Hebrew Missionary College; and I must confess I was extremely glad when I received the following letters from the Committee :—

"LONDON SOCIETY FOR PROMOTING CHRISTIANITY AMONGST THE JEWS.

"16 LINCOLN'S INN FIELDS,
"LONDON, W.C., 24th September, 1877.

"DEAR SIR,—The Committee having considered your case on Friday last, decided that you should now see the clerical examiners; and arrangements have been made for you to call upon two of them, as follows—viz., Rev. H. A. Stern, on Wednesday next, between three and four o'clock ; and, Rev. John Richardson, 169 The Grove, Camberwell, on Thursday next, at 4.30.

" Please be punctual in your attendance upon them at the times mentioned.

" Wishing you a pleasant and satisfactory interview.—I remain yours faithfully,

"W. J. ADAMS,
"*Assistant Secy.*"

"LONDON SOCIETY FOR PROMOTING CHRISTIANITY AMONGST THE JEWS.

"16 LINCOLN'S INN FIELDS,
"LONDON, W.C., 5th October, 1877.

"DEAR SIR,—Be good enough to attend on another examiner, the Rev. J. Kirkman, 4 Thurlow Road, Hampstead, on Tuesday morning next, at eleven A.M.—With best wishes, I remain, yours faithfully,

"W. J. ADAMS."

CHAPTER XVI.

APPOINTMENT AS JEWISH MISSIONARY; FIRST VISIT TO SCOTLAND; LETTER FROM REV. J. G. CUNNINGHAM; TRANSFERRED FROM LONDON TO BUCHAREST; MY FIRST MISSION JOURNEYS IN ROUMANIA; PREACHING THE GOSPEL IN A PECULIAR WAY TO THOUSANDS OF JEWS; MY WINTER WORK IN BUCHAREST; THE PRESENT JEWISH CEREMONY OF THE PASSOVER NIGHTS AS A CHRISTIAN SYMBOL; A LETTER FROM THE PRINCIPAL OF THE HEBREW MISSIONARY COLLEGE.

ON the ninth of October, I passed my last clerical examination, and on the 12th I was appointed by the Society to labour for a short time in London, until the Committee should find a proper station for me. In August, 1878, I paid my first visit to Scotland. On my arrival, in the evening, in Edinburgh, I went to the Edinburgh Hotel, and the next day I called upon Dr. Moody Stuart, to whom I had a letter of introduction from Rev. W. Wingate; but the Doctor was out of town, and I was told by the servant that if I wanted any information, I could obtain it from the Rev. J. G. Cunningham. I went, therefore, to 7 Brandon Street, and found in the above-named gentleman, a most warm-hearted brother in Christ. He did not allow me to remain in the hotel, but took me to his house, where I stayed for a week, during which time he introduced me to many

Christian friends, as also to the Jewish Mission Committee of the Free Church of Scotland. I was glad to have an opportunity of expressing my hearty thanks to the Committee for sending missionaries to the Jews, through whose instrumentality I was brought to Christ. I also told them that my heart's desire ever since, had been to labour in connection with the same Church and Mission which had been the means of my becoming a Christian, and that I should be glad at any time when the Committee should wish to employ me, to enter into their service. They were very glad to hear this, and replied that they should be glad to have me in their service.

After spending sixteen days in Scotland, a week in Edinburgh and a week in Portobello, with Mrs. Morice, the aunt of Mrs. Tomory, who invited me to stay with her, and two days in Helensburgh with Mrs. Fleming, who also invited me, I returned to London, where I found a resolution passed by the Committee appointing me as missionary to Bucharest in Roumania.

As it was my great desire to be connected with the Free Church, and my meeting with the Jewish Mission Committee in Edinburgh gave me some hope of my wishes being realised, I did not accept the appointment to Bucharest, until I had received the following letter from Rev. J. G. Cunningham, minister of St. Luke's, in Edinburgh.

"7 BRANDON STREET, 12th *August*, 1878.

"MY DEAR FRIEND,—Your kind letter came to me on Saturday, when I was too busy to answer it at once. It has been often in my mind since, and I pray the Lord to guide you to the right course. I have been remembering, in connection with your present case, Numbers ix. 17-23. We may not stay behind when the cloud of His presence moves forward, and we may not go before the cloud. It seems to me, that in the circumstance that our Committee have meanwhile no access to Russia, and no intention of occupying Palestine, the way is left open for you to accept the call to Bucharest, in giving which, the Committee have indicated in a very satisfactory way their confidence in you. The visit you paid to Scotland has made you some warm friends, who will take a sincere interest in your work and welfare wherever you may be ; and I am sure they share your feeling, that it would be especially pleasant for you to work in connection with the Church by which you were first brought to the knowledge of our Saviour. For this, however, as I have indicated above, the way does not seem, in the meantime, to be open. We look back with very great pleasure on your visit to us, and I only regret that my constant work at the time prevented me from taking you to visit places of interest in our beautiful city.

I send you a copy of the " Notes for Teachers " for this month, which I was busy writing when you were here.

With kind regards from Mrs. Cunningham, and hoping to hear again from you,—I remain, my dear Mr. Bassin, yours sincerely,

J. G. CUNNINGHAM."

I then left for Bucharest, and in October, 1878, I made my first missionary journey in Roumania, accompanied by a colporteur. The first town we visited was Galatz, on the river Danube, where we remained for two days, and had the opportunity of preaching the Gospel to some hundred of Jews in the streets.

The second town was Berlad, where we remained for three weeks. I arranged my work in that town as follows : Day by day I accompanied the colporteur from house to house. He sold the Bibles and tracts, and I preached the Gospel. On the Jewish Sabbath I had a service in Hebrew and a sermon in German. The attendance was very good, and the Jews listened attentively. They also joined in our prayers, and repeated the psalms for the day with us, according to the custom of the Episcopal Church. On the first Saturday, the Hebrew prayers made such an impression upon them that they said afterwards to their Jewish brethren who did not attend my first meeting, that the missionary prays very well in the holy tongue. This announcement brought me many Jews the next Saturday, so that the jealousy of the more bigoted Jews was aroused, and they invited a great Jewish preacher from another town to preach against me. My colporteur, who first heard of it, came and told me he was afraid we should have no listeners next Saturday, as the Jewish preacher will preach at the same hour as is announced for our service. "Never mind," I replied, "we have time to give out our service for an hour before." I then announced immediately that our service would be held at 2 P.M. instead of 3 P.M., and as I made this known on the Friday afternoon, the Jewish preacher had no time to alter his hour, consequently the attendance at my service on that Saturday was as good as on the two previous ones. When I had finished my lecture, I went with the Jews of my own meeting to the synagogue to hear my opponent. As soon as I entered, the whole congregation turned their faces towards me, and in a little while some asked my opinion of the preaching. I did not wish to reply in the synagogue, so I went out of it, whereupon the congregation left their preacher and followed me. Outside, in the open air, I took the Jewish preacher's text, which was from Genesis vi. 9: "Noah was a just man, and perfect in his generations;

and Noah walked with God." I was soon surrounded by some thousands of Jews, who came out of the several synagogues which were in that synagogue court (frequently several synagogues are erected round one large court); and as it was the time of offering the afternoon prayers, they were all crowded. No sooner was it known that I was preaching than the congregations hastened to hear what I might have to say. Two strong lusty Jews lifted me up, and kept me on their arms, until a chair was brought, upon which I stood, in order to be seen by the whole assembly. I preached for more than two hours, and when I went home, some of the Jews accompanied me to my lodgings.

During the three weeks I was in Berlad, many Jews came daily to me to hear the Gospel truths. When I left that town for Bucharest, many of them came even to the station. I had just cause to thank the Lord for accounting me worthy to preach the Gospel to so many of my own nation.

In the beginning of November, 1878, I arrived in Bucharest from my first missionary journey. My next work was to introduce Hebrew into the mission school, and for some time I instructed the children in my most beloved language. The winter of 1879 I spent in Bucharest, visiting the Jews in their houses, restaurants, cafés, places of business, and synagogues. On Saturdays, I preached to the Jews in the mission chapel. During this winter I made many friends among the Jews, who used to invite me to their houses, and were glad to see me every day. I was invited by one of them to spend the first night of the Feast of the Passover, when the ceremony is performed, which I have already described in chapter xiv. of the first part of this book. After the ceremony was performed, my friend, Mr. Lichtenblau, asked me what I thought of it. "But do you understand what you are doing?" I asked of my host. His answer was, "I believe I do." "Then tell me, friend," I said, "what is the meaning of the three cakes, the breaking of the middle one, and putting it between the cushions? And, after partaking of supper you remove the cake again and distribute a piece of it to each of the company, who eat it with great solemnity." "I do not know," was his reply, "and I would like to hear from you what you think of it."

I then addressed myself to all who were assembled at the table, and said, "This ceremony is more suitable for Christians than for the modern Jews, for they find something typical in it. The three cakes are symbolical of God—the Father, the Son, and the Holy Ghost. The middle cake represents the Son of God, who revealed Himself in a human body; that body was broken for the salvation of mankind, and put into the grave for a little while. The taking out the cake from under the cushion, before you drink the third cup of wine, is a symbol of the broken body which rose from the grave in the beginning of the third day. The distribution of a piece of it to each of the company is symbolic of what Christ said: 'Take and eat it in remembrance of My body which was broken for you.'"

The company expressed great astonishment at my explanation, and Mr. Lichtenblau said: "You explain everything in connection with the Christian doctrine."

"But have you any other explanation of it," I asked him. "No," he replied. He then inquired how it came among the Jews, to which I answered : "Probably through secret Hebrew Christians, who were greatly honoured by the Jews, who have imitated what the Christians did."

I was encouraged in my work, not only because I found a wide open door among the Jews, but also because of the sympathy of Christian friends in England, of which the following letter from the Principal of the Hebrew Missionary College is a specimen :—

"LONDON SOCIETY FOR PROMOTING CHRISTIANITY AMONG THE JEWS.

"HEBREW MISSIONARY COLLEGE,
"*9th January*, 1879.

"MY DEAR MR. BASSIN,—I cannot allow the New Year to pass without sending you my good wishes in the Lord, for yourself, and the continued success of your work. May He who has brought you hitherto, continue to lead and bless you with all temporal and spiritual blessings in Christ Jesus. I rejoice to hear from you, that your work is prospering. May it continue so, and may you increase and abound therein.

"Our preparatory work in the College is still going on, I trust with profit. We are endeavouring just now to fix and deepen it, in order to make it more directly useful to the Mission. We have had no change in our members yet, but Mr. Wertheim expects to leave us very soon. So, by degrees, will one and another go forth from us, carrying with him the prayers and good wishes of those whom he leaves behind, and not less praying for them in his turn. I would ask you also to remember us in this way. Without the help of the Lord we can do nothing; therefore pray for us.

"I hope you still keep up your studies as much as possible. Depend upon it, you will not find the time wasted. For the cultivation of your own mind, as well as for the success of your work, they are most valuable. If I can be of any assistance to you therein, it will afford me great pleasure.

"I am glad to find from your letter that you like your work. You will doubtless meet with much to discourage you, but patient continuance in well doing must in the end secure its reward. In the Lord's own time the Spirit shall be poured out from on high. If you are not able to do much in the way of actual conversion, you are leavening the Jewish mind, and some day the results will be seen. If you are not labouring for yourself, you are for your successors. One soweth and another reapeth. If your task is to sow, patiently fulfil it, remembering the promise: 'They that sow in tears shall reap in joy.'

"We all unite in the expression of our good wishes.—Yours, very faithfully,

"H. SYMMONS."*

* By Principal Symmons's death on 22nd January, 1880, I lost a warm friend.

CHAPTER XVII.

MY SECOND AND THIRD MISSIONARY JOURNEYS IN ROUMANIA; MY RETURN TO LONDON; CORRESPONDENCE WITH THE JEWISH MISSION COMMITTEE OF THE FREE CHURCH OF SCOTLAND; MY SECOND VISIT TO SCOTLAND.

IN May, 1879, I made my second missionary journey in Roumania. The first town I visited was Brahilo, a free and chief shipping port of Wallachia on the left bank of the Danube, about 100 miles from its mouth, with a population of about 40,000, including several thousands of Jews. There I met one of our colporteurs, who was awaiting me. I found that Brahilo was not a good place for a Jewish mission, and as I knew there were better places, where the Jews were more willing to listen to the Gospel, I remained there only four days, and then left for Galatz, accompanied by the colporteur.

Galatz is the chief port town of Moldavia, and the centre of the commerce of the whole kingdom of Roumania. It is situated on the left bank of the Danube, about 93 miles from its mouth. The population is about 80,000, of which about 20,000 are Jews. Here I found very interesting work among the Jews, and preached the Gospel to them in their houses, in their synagogues, and in their places of business. Many of them also attended my services in the German Protestant Church. After working there for a fortnight, I went to Tulza, leaving the colporteur in Galatz. Tulza is the chief town of the region Dobrudscha, which belongs to Roumania since 1878, and is situated on the right bank of the Danube, at the commencement of the Delta. The population is about 6000, comprising Bulgarians, Roumanians, Tartars, Turks, Greeks, Armenians, Russians, Germans, and about 1000 Jews. I stayed ten days in Tulza, preaching the Gospel in Russian and in German to Jews and Gentiles. One most interesting case I met with was that of a Russian who had been a Christian, but became a Jew some years ago. I had a very interesting discourse with him. I showed him the difference between us. "He was-born of Christian parents, and brought up in the Greek Church; but through his ignorance of the Christian truths he became a Jew. I was born of Jewish parents, and brought up as a rabbi; but I became a Christian through knowledge of the Word of God. I was a learned Jew, and now I am a learned Christian; he was an ignorant Christian, and is now an ignorant Jew. I have hope of everlasting life through the blood of Christ, which cleanses me from all my sin; he must die in his sins and be lost for ever. Oh! how terrible the thought," said I to him; but though he wept, he made no reply to my daily entreaties with him.

From Tulza I returned to Galatz for five days, proceeding thence in company with the colporteur to Fokschan. This town is divided by the stream,

Milkow, into two parts, the west part belonging to Wallachia, the east to Moldavia; the population is about 25,000, of which about 8000 are Jews. I remained there for two weeks, and had very good opportunities for preaching the Gospel to many Jews in their houses, and in the synagogues. I also held services in the house of a Christian friend, which were well attended by the Jews. The chief rabbi, though very friendly when I visited him, declined to enter into a religious conversation.

From Fokschan we went to Rimnik Sarat, where I had a glorious opportunity of proclaiming the word of salvation to the Jews. We remained for twelve days, and I was more honoured by the Jews there, than in any other town I had previously visited, and for this reason: The second day after our arrival was a Friday, the day on which the Jews are accustomed to go into a bath to purify themselves for the coming Sabbath; so I went there also, and met with the chief rabbi, who, after we had exchanged a few words, asked me if I were the missionary of whose arrival he had heard. On my replying in the affirmative, he requested me to speak in Hebrew with him, in order that the populace might not understand our conversation. After a long conversation in Hebrew, he invited me to his house, where we discoursed day by day for hours, in the presence of many Jews. When I left him, he spoke very highly of me, and this opened a wide door to me amongst the Jews. Whenever I met one in the street, he saluted me most cordially. In the synagogues I could preach the Gospel freely, and when I was leaving the town, the rabbi gave me an introduction to his son, who was director of the Jewish school in Buzu, the next town that we were going to.

We stayed two days only in Buzu, and then continued our journey to Plojeschti. On the way there I met with a railway accident, in which I was sufficiently hurt to be obliged to keep my bed for a few days after our arrival in Plojeschti. As soon as I was better, I began my work amongst the Jews, and was assisted by the Hungarian Reformed pastor, who lent his church for me to hold my services in, and to preach to the Jews. Plojeschti is a town in the interior of Wallachia; it has a population of about 30,000, of which about 5000 are Jews. I stayed there for two weeks, and made many friends amongst the Jews, who also invited me into their houses, in order to have religious conversation with me.

From this town I returned to Bucharest, from whence, after a few weeks, I set out upon my third missionary journey.

Krajova is the chief town of Little Wallachia, 120 miles west of Bucharest; it is the residence of many rich bojars, *i.e.*, Roumanian nobles. The population, about 28,000, included about 4000 Jews, the most of whom are Spanish Jews. I found the work there so interesting that I remained for more than a month. My services in the German Protestant church were attended by crowds of Jews; the chief rabbi of the Spanish community and I visited each other daily. The rabbi of the Polish Jewish community received me in a very friendly manner, but did not like to enter into religious conversation. The chief rabbi of the Spanish Jews gave me his likeness, and wrote upon it, in Hebrew, as follows: "A gift of everlasting remembrance to the beloved of my soul, the honoured doctor, Elieser Bassin—his light shall shine for ever—from his sincere friend Zacharia Levi."

From Krajova I went to Turn-Severin, where I spent five weeks preaching the Gospel to the Jews. On Sunday mornings I used to preach for the German Protestant pastor, and in the afternoon I had a special service to the Jews in the same church; the morning service was in German, the afternoon service in Hebrew.

In October, 1879, I returned again to Bucharest, and in the retrospect of my three journeys I could, with joy and thanksgiving to God, express my deep conviction that Roumania presents a most encouraging field for Jewish mission operations.

Gladly would I have remained in that important mission field, but in consequence of misunderstandings which arose between me and the head of the Mission, Rev. J. F. Kleinhenn, and of other reasons, which though it might interest the reader to know them, yet this is not the place for recording them, I resigned my connection with the London Society for promoting Christianity among the Jews.

In December, 1879, I returned to London, and entered into correspondence with the Jewish Mission Committee of the Free Church of Scotland, and in January, 1880, I received the following letter:—

"7 BRANDON STREET,
"EDINBURGH, 14th *January*, 1880.

"MY DEAR SIR,—I duly received your letter, and was very glad to hear from you again. I am so busy that I delayed answering your letter until I should have an opportunity of laying it before our Committee. It does not meet till the 20th inst., but I have told a few of them about your wish to be in the service of the Committee. These friends wished to know whether any person interested in Jewish Missions could *with safety* go into Russia at this time, and begin any such work in any place such as Moscow. Do you know how this stands at the present time?

"So far as I see, the Committee have no opening for you just now, but *perhaps* they might, if they could begin to do anything in Russia; as yet, however, they have done nothing.

"I hope that the Lord may open up your way.

"With kind regards, and hoping to hear from you about Russia as a field of Jewish Missions,—I remain, my dear Sir, yours most sincerely,

"J. G. CUNNINGHAM."

My reply to this letter was that there was no opening in Russia for a Mission just then, but that Moldavia presented a wide open door, and a large field for labour amongst the Jews. To this proposal I received the following answer:—

"7 BRANDON STREET,
"EDINBURGH, 18*th February*, 1880.

"MY DEAR SIR,—I am sorry to keep you so long in suspense. The Committee appointed to consider the question of a Mission to the Moldavian Jews has not yet been called together. I will, as soon as they meet, mention your willingness to come to Edinburgh, to give information on the subject, and will let you know whether they will send for you or not for this purpose. I wish that they would.

"I trust that you are well. I am sorry you should be so long without work, but I hope something will soon open to you.—I am, my dear Sir, your brother in Christ,

"J. G. CUNNINGHAM."

In the meantime I accepted temporary employment from the Society whose service I had resigned in

Roumania. I could have had permanent occupation in their Mission had I wished it. But besides other reasons, the hope of entering the service of the Free Church kept me back from submitting to some strange rules of the London Jewish Mission Society. This hope was strengthened by the following letter:—

"7 BRANDON STREET,
"EDINBURGH, 1st *May*, 1880.

"MY DEAR SIR,—I am sorry that I have been hindered by pressure of other matters constantly from writing earlier to you, but you have been much and affectionately remembered. Will you be so good as to call upon the Secretary of the London Society by which you were sent to Bucharest, or communicate with him, so as to obtain in writing from him a few lines as to the circumstances of your ceasing to be employed by the Society. I have some hope of finding something for you to do in connection with our Mission, and personally I am satisfied that you did your duty faithfully in the other Society's service. But for our Committee it would be necessary to have a certificate, regarding your resignation, from the Secretary of the London Society.

"Hoping that you will kindly attend to this without delay,—I remain, my dear Sir, yours most sincerely,

"J. G. CUNNINGHAM."

After this letter, I entertained great hopes of entering the service of the Church to which I owe so much; but I was rather disappointed by the following communication:—

"7 BRANDON STREET,
"EDINBURGH, 29th *June*, 1880.

"MY DEAR SIR,—I received your letter, and also a letter of recommendation from the Secretary of the London Society, and we have, besides these, good accounts of you from Mr. Wingate. I laid the information before the Committee, and it was received with interest; but as the Committee, though very desirous to have a mission in Roumania, will not undertake it until a Scotch missionary be found to take charge of it, I am sorry to say that there is no opening meanwhile for you, which is a matter of sincere regret to us all. I hope for a change in this before long meanwhile it is a painful disappointment. May the Lord help you to bear it, and soon open up your way!

"With kind regards and sincere esteem, I am, my dear friend, yours sincerely,   "J. G. CUNNINGHAM."

This determined me to go to Edinburgh, in order to see the Committee myself. Accordingly I went there in July, 1880. I found my friend, Rev. J. G. Cunningham, was out of town; so I paid a visit to Dr. J. H. Wilson, of the Barclay Church. He was extremely kind to me, and invited me to stay with him. My way was not clear before me at that time, and both Dr. and Mrs. Wilson comforted me greatly. When shown to my room, my eye fell upon a text full of comfort, which was hung upon the wall; it was from Ps. lv. 22: "Cast thy burden upon the Lord, and He shall sustain thee."

CHAPTER XVIII.

APPOINTED BY THE FREE CHURCH OF SCOTLAND TO VISIT ROUMANIA; INVITATION FROM W. HENDERSON, ESQ., TO VISIT ABERDEEN; LETTERS OF CONGRATULATION UPON MY APPOINTMENT FROM REV. W. WINGATE, REV. DR. STERN, REV. J. B. BARRACLOUGH, ASSISTANT SECRETARY OF THE LONDON JEWISH MISSION SOCIETY, AND FROM REV. J. G. CUNNINGHAM; MY VISITS TO GREENOCK AND TO LEITH; LETTER FROM REV. J. THOMPSON; STARTING FOR ROUMANIA; ADDRESS TO THE JEWS IN BRESLAU; ARRIVAL IN JASSY.

AT the meeting of the Jewish Mission Committee of the Free Church of Scotland in July, 1880, I was appointed to visit Roumania, and to spend one year there in the work of proclaiming the Gospel to my Jewish brethren (more particularly in Jassy), and to report to the Committee as to the expediency and hopefulness of establishing a permanent mission station in that country.

I need hardly say how happy this appointment made me, and that it also gave pleasure to my Christian friends will be seen from the following letters:—

"DEVANHA HOUSE,
"ABERDEEN, 22nd July, 1880.

"MY DEAR SIR,—I have your note of yesterday, and I am very glad to hear that you have at length got into the service of the Free Church. I trust the Lord will make you useful in leading many to a knowledge of the truth in the Gospel of Jesus Christ.

"Mrs. Henderson and I will be very pleased and glad to see you in Aberdeen, and we will be at home from the 27th of this month until the 2nd of August. If you could, therefore, come north at that time, we will be delighted to see you.—I am, yours sincerely, "WM. HENDERSON."

On my arrival in Aberdeen, I was very cordially met at the station by Mr. Henderson, who conveyed me in a carriage to his residence, where I was received with the same cordiality by Mrs. Henderson and family. During my stay in Aberdeen I received the following congratulatory letters from my friends:—

"100 TALBOT ROAD, BAYSWATER,
"LONDON, 24th July, 1880.

"MY DEAR ELIESER,—After delays to try faith and patience you have got 'your heart's desire.' I sincerely sympathise with you, and congratulate you on your appointment to carry the Gospel to your brethren, and to all men, as a missionary of the Free Church of Scotland. You will now have thorough sympathy and co-operation in your work, and need no other rule save the Holy Spirit and the Word of God for guidance.

"May the many prayers which have gone up in your behalf be abundantly answered in grace for all to which you are now called. Make the Epistles to Timothy and Titus a special study; and may you be used to the salvation of many! If you come *via* London, come and see us. You are graciously dealt with, in having so many ministers of Christ to befriend you.

"Mrs. Wingate joins me in kindest remembrances.—Yours sincerely, "WILLIAM WINGATE."

"5 CAMBRIDGE LODGE VILLAS,
"MARE STREET, E., *August* 2.

"MY DEAR MR. BASSIN,—I write a line to thank you for your note. It affords me great pleasure to hear that you have been appointed as missionary of the Free Church of Scotland. May the blessing which cometh from above rest upon your future career! You know something of the work, and are also acquainted with its difficulties and trials, hopes and promises. From my own experience, I know that our labours, if carried on in the strength of the Lord, cannot and will not fail to redound to His glory.

"I am glad to hear that 'Elieser' is becoming known in Scotland. May your sacrifices for the Gospel's sake stir up much interest in behalf of our people.—With Christian regards, faithfully yours,

"HENRY A. STERN."

"LONDON SOCIETY FOR PROMOTING CHRISTIANITY AMONGST THE JEWS.

"16 LINCOLN'S INN FIELDS,
"LONDON, W.C., 3rd August, 1880.

"DEAR MR. BASSIN,—We are glad to hear of your appointment. May the Lord bless you, and make you a blessing in your new sphere of work for Him!

"Mr. Kleinhenn is not now in London. His present address is—Care of Thos. Blyth, Esq., The Fields, Southam, Warwickshire. —Believe me, faithfully yours,

"J. B. BARRACLOUGH,
"*Assistant Secretary.*"

"7 BRANDON STREET,
"EDINBURGH, 6th August, 1880.

"MY DEAR SIR,—I was truly glad to receive at Strathpeffer the intimation of your being appointed to visit Roumania, in the service of our Jewish Mission. It is what I did earnestly desire to hear. May God guide you and bless you in the work, and in all your way! Gen. xxiv. 27.

"I am also very glad to hear of your being with Mr. Henderson, a true and generous friend of Israel. Will you remember me kindly to him?

"When you come to Edinburgh, please let me know, and if I

have no room in my own house unoccupied, I will try to find one for you in some other friend's.—Believe me, my dear Sir, yours most sincerely,

"J. G. CUNNINGHAM."

During my two weeks' stay in the north of Scotland, Mr. and Mrs. Henderson showed me such true Christian love, that I had not words enough to thank them. They not only introduced me to many Christian friends in Aberdeen, but they also took me into the country where they had been invited, and I enjoyed two very happy days with them in Aberdour, at Mr. Barclay's. When arrangements had been made for me to preach in Ferryhill Free Church, on Sabbath, 1st August, Mr. and Mrs. Henderson took great pains to make it known far and wide; they printed intimations and sent them to all the ministers, and to many Christian friends. They also arranged that I should preach in their son's church at Insch.

In the west of Scotland, also, I enjoyed the warm fellowship of Christian friends. In Greenock, Provost Campbell showed me great Christian love. When it had been arranged that I should preach on Sabbath, 15th August, in the morning, in the Rev. J. J. Bonar's church, and in the afternoon, in the Rev. Dr. William Laughton's, he had bills printed and circulated on his own account, in order to give me encouragement in proclaiming the lovingkindness and tender mercies of our blessed Lord Jesus Christ.

Before leaving Scotland to commence my missionary tour, I addressed Dr. Horatius Bonar's congregation, and asked them to accompany me with their prayers, and I believe many did so. On the last Sabbath,

22nd August, I conducted Divine service in Free St. Ninian's Church, Leith. In remembrance of my late friend and active member of the Jewish Mission Committee, Rev. John Thomson, M.A., I shall here insert a letter which he wrote to me:—

"150 FERRY ROAD,
"LEITH, 20th *August*, 1880.

"MY DEAR SIR,—It will give me very great pleasure to have you preach in my church in the afternoon of Sabbath next, the 22nd August.

"I have just come home, and have only time to say this before post.

"Hoping to see you here at about half-past one o'clock,—I am my dear Sir, yours very truly,

"J. THOMSON."

On the 24th August, 1880, I left Scotland, and after spending a week in London, I set out upon my journey to Roumania, by steamer to Hamburg, and thence by train through Berlin to Breslau, where I stayed for a few days, and preached in Rev. Daniel Edward's place of worship to a crowded congregation of Jews and Christians. Some of the younger Jews became much excited, and, after the address, expressed their desire to speak to me. We had a very warm discourse, in which Mr. Edward took a lively part. Miss Edward told us that she heard a Jewess asking a Jew if it was really true—what I had quoted from the prayers which they use on Friday evenings on the eve of their Sabbath—"Through the Son of Jesse of Bethlehem, draw near to my soul and deliver it."

From Breslau I proceeded by train through Lemberg and Tsherowitz to Jassy, arriving in the Moldavian capital, 12th September, 1880.

CHAPTER XIX.

COMMENCEMENT OF MISSION WORK IN JASSY; EVENING RELIGIOUS DISCOURSES—FIRST IN MR. FOLTICINEANO'S HOUSE, THEN IN MY OWN; THE MISSION ROOM; THE EVENING BIBLE CLASS; SATURDAY LECTURES; MY REPORT TO THE GENERAL ASSEMBLY OF 1881; REV. D. EDWARD VISITS JASSY; HIS REPORT TO THE COMMITTEE, AND SUBSEQUENT LETTER TO ME.

THE day after my arrival in Jassy, I went out to see the Jews, and met with some of them whose acquaintance I had made during my journeys in Roumania in 1878 and 1879. They were very glad to see me again, and introduced me to some Jewish families. Afterwards I went into the coffee-houses and restaurants, in order to make further acquaintance with Jews. In one of these I had not long to wait before it became known that I was a missionary, and then I was assailed with religious questions. These, however, I would not answer in the coffee-house, knowing that if I did so, a noisy controversy would ensue, at which the keeper of the house would be displeased. So I only replied: "Dear friends, I would gladly answer you, but this is not the place for it. However, if you really wish me to answer you, come to my house at any time that suits you, or invite me to yours, and I am ready to give you the information you desire;"

whereupon Mr. Folticineano proposed that we should withdraw to his house, which was only across the street. To this all agreed, and the conversation was continued there until eleven in the evening. It was arranged that the next meeting on the following evening should be at my house, from eight till eleven o'clock. The company, comprising nine, came punctually to the appointed hour, some of them bringing friends also. The discourse was a very lively one, and soon began to get very confusing also, for I had scarcely time to answer one question before five or six others were put to me. So I was obliged to remind them that our discourses would not profit us, if carried on in such confusion, and suggested that we should take up the questions one by one. To this all agreed, so that for the future our meetings were much quieter and more orderly.

After a few weeks I obtained a mission-room which served us for a reading-room through the day, a Bible class-room in the evening, and a lecture-room on Saturdays. The first lecture I gave was on Lev. xvii. 11. It was a treatise from the rabbinical books on the signification of the sacrifice and of the blood of the covenant. At the close, I announced that on the following Saturday we would (*D.V.*) consider the cause of the destruction of the temple and the cessation of the sacrifices; also the means whereby in these days we may find redemption for our souls. At the end of the second lecture, I intimated that the third would treat of the Messiah, as to whether He has come or is yet to come. The fourth lecture proved to them that Jesus is the Messiah; the fifth that He is

s

seated at God's right hand; and the sixth showed why the Jews rejected Him.

I published the first lecture in the Hebrew and Roumanian languages, and would have published the other five also, as the first was so well received by the Jews, but my means would not allow of it. The impression which these lectures made upon the Jews will be seen from the following report to the Committee for the General Assembly in 1881 :—

"The station from which I write this report has a place in the very early date of the history of the Free Church of Scotland, but for more than thirty years this station was not occupied by our Church after Rev. D. Edward left it in 1848, on account of the unsafe state in which the country was at that time. It was a chief station in the time of Mr. Edward, now in Breslau. Years have passed on, the Episcopalians occupied it, but it never recovered to be as before; and through some disaster to the missionaries, the place was left, and has been unoccupied for some years.

"Since Mr. Edward left Jassy, that place and the land have undergone great political changes. (1) The union of the two Danubian Principalities, Wallachia and Moldavia, in one Roumania in 1859; (2) the Constitution of 1866; and (3) the Independence of 1878. In May next, the prince of this country—Charles the First—will be proclaimed the first king of Roumania.

"By the providence of God, I was appointed by the Jewish Mission Committee, 20th July, 1880, to visit Roumania in order that, after spending one year in the work of making known the Gospel among my Jewish brethren, I might report as to the expediency and hopefulness of establishing a permanent Jewish mission station in this country, which I now do accordingly.

"The number of Jews in Jassy amounts to about 50,000. Of this large number many are bankers, merchants, and hold different professional appointments; but the majority are poor, and many in such a miserable condition as is scarcely equalled in any other place in Europe. The Jews here are divided into three sects—

(1) Talmudists, (2) Chasidim, and (3) Lemi-Reformer. But I find no difficulty in getting into contact with any of them, as they are for the most part not averse to religious discussion. There is one thing of great importance and significance—that among all classes so many are dissatisfied with Judaism, and desire a better faith. As soon as my arrival here became known, several young Jews came to me expressing their desire for instruction in the Christian religion, and some even for baptism.

"It is now about nine months since I duly commenced mission work here, and on reviewing the same I can with pleasure and thankfulness to God express my deep conviction that Moldavia presents a most encouraging field for Jewish mission operations.

"My lectures have attracted not only hearers and readers, but also the envy of the rabbis and orthodox Jews, who tried to counteract my work, but in vain. The articles which they wrote in their papers to warn the Jews brought me more hearers, so that amidst all the difficulties I had to contend with, I feel there is much cause to bless the Lord for the progress which has been made in the short time I have been here, and that the barriers which Satan raises are but as cobweb walls, impotent to withstand fervent prayer and faithful labour. 'If the Lord be for us, who can be against us.'

"The Jews in this country are more hopeful and promising than those in any other where I have as yet been.

"Since my public lectures, and distribution of them amongst those who did not hear them, I marked a growing consciousness that a religion professing to be Divine must be able to satisfy man's highest aspirations. They saw from the lectures that the present Judaism cannot do it, and many asked me what they were to do? The great difficulty is that they do not like to secede from the synagogue, and break the feeble tie that binds them to their people. I know here many Jews who are persuaded that Jesus is the Messiah, but notwithstanding this conviction, will not openly profess the faith they secretly cherish. Gladly would they do so, did they not shrink from the sacrifices such a step would entail.

"Besides the special lectures, I held also evening Bible classes, and had a daily reading-room; and I hope it has been a blessing to many of the house of Israel.

"Since I came here, fourteen Jews have presented themselves for instruction and baptism. Eight of them appeared to me to be wanting in earnestness; but not deeming it right to refuse them at once, I encouraged their visits, in order that I might form a better opinion of their fitness. These visits continued for some time, but when they found that I had no temporal advantages to offer, they ultimately withdrew. With two others I had similar experience. They came almost every day for some weeks, in order, they said, to dispute and debate, and often used very hostile language. However, they soon ceased to dispute and became silent listeners, and at last offered themselves as candidates for baptism. This quite perplexed me, as I could scarcely believe that such a thorough change of mind could have taken place in so short a time. This I candidly explained to them, and said that although I did not doubt their sincerity, I thought it best there should be some time longer before baptism. They then went away, and have not since called upon me. Three I have still under instruction, of whom I have also great hope that the Lord will bring them to His flock. One who was a candidate for baptism left Jassy for Vienna, on account of the death of his father there.

"The Jews desire very much to have a school. Many have several times asked me if I am going to have any, for they like the mission schools very much; and the late mission school is still remembered with gratitude by many. I shall be extremely happy if our Church will resolve to establish a school here, where the name of Jesus should be heard, read, and sung. I feel sure that to many it would be a sweet sound, and seed that may bring forth fruit a hundred-fold.

"In conclusion, I can only express my thankfulness to the Almighty God, through our Lord Jesus Christ, for the many opportunities of preaching His Word which have been vouchsafed to me; and I will go on casting out the seed, in the hope of reaping in due time, trusting in God's gracious promise that His Word shall not return void. May the Lord who in His providence placed me here, and who is able and willing to do abundantly more than we can ask or think, pour out the Holy Spirit, and give His grace and wisdom to all who are engaged in making known His glory to his ancient people Israel."

After the General Assembly of 1881, the Jewish Mission Committee desired Rev. D. Edward to visit me, and then to come to Edinburgh and report personally as to the hopefulness of establishing a permanent mission station in Roumania.

Mr. Edward, accordingly, came to Jassy about the beginning of July 1881. He expressed great delight at finding the better class of the Jews attending the Saturday meetings, and evidently such attentive hearers, and so friendly disposed towards me. To the Committee he gave a most favourable report of the work, as well as of the place, as being a very hopeful field for a mission to the Jews, as may be seen from the following letter which he subsequently wrote to me:—

"BRESLAU, 27th *August*, 1881.

" DEAR MR. BASSIN,—You are doubtless impatient to hear my report how your case was treated in the Committee, but I could not write earlier, as I have had so many papers to prepare for different committees.

"Well, I reported to the Committee just as I expressed myself when with you, especially setting forth that you had Jews attending in considerable numbers at your lectures, and that you had succeeded in getting the Jews' papers to notice your work. I did not conceal that I regarded these as great achievements. . . . . I think I set forth all your work and claims as favourably as I could. Of course, when the Committee were of opinion that if they proceeded to grant sanction for a school or operative institution, they would require to have a British (Scotch) missionary appointed by your side, I could not object ; indeed, I consider this every way desirable, if it can be had, for yourself as well as for the mission. You have had your whole case set before the Committee in the most advantageous manner, but there is one thing needful, that the Committee know you better. You are conscious of your own singleness of purpose, and may be displeased that the Committee has not at once full confidence in you (and I, *for my part*, have no doubt that you desire above all things the Lord's glory). But you can only get general credit for this by patient working. Let me advise you to go on seeking the advancement of Christ's work in Israel, seeking the conversion of souls, and in a short time you will obtain all that is for the welfare of the cause, as well as for your own comfort. The Lord is evidently calling you to patience; ask of the Almighty to bestow this grace upon you; humble yourself under His mighty hand, and He will look upon you to bless you.

"In especial, I would advise you to confine yourself to special work, and forbear from engaging in large and general speculations and enterprises, for this will only create a prejudice against you.

"I have not seen Dr. M. Stuart at all, though he wrote to me, excusing himself on the score of ill-health, but those to whom I spoke of your wish . . . all thought you should *wait*. Seek grace then, dear friend, to wait God's time for this or every step —our waiting upon God (Ps. xxvii. 14), He is ready and able to honour in due season. . . .—Affectionately yours in Christ.

"D. EDWARD."

CHAPTER XX.

CIRCULAR TO THE LEARNED JEWS AND CHRISTIANS CONCERNING THE JEWISH QUESTION; SUGGESTIONS FOR THE SOLVING OF THE JEWISH QUESTION; ANSWERS TO MY CIRCULAR FROM DR. FÜRST, DR. PAULUS CASSEL, MR. BUTYNSKI OF RUSSIA, AND PROFESSOR DR. DELITZSCH.

SORROW at hearing of the disgraceful persecution of my Jewish brethren in Russia, the shameful agitation in Germany, and seeing the bad treatment which they receive in Roumania, moved me to issue, in May, 1881, a circular in which I requested the learned world to give their opinion as to what practical methods could be adopted for bringing about a reconciliation between Jews and Christians, so that the one should be a blessing to the other.

It is well known that nothing in the world can take place without leaving impressions—upon some good, upon others bad. Such was the case with my circular also; no sooner had it been issued than answers were abundantly sent in,—some favourable, some unfavourable,—but the latter did not discourage me. I resolved to publish them in pamphlets, together with my own suggestions, as follows:—

I. The case of the Jewish question must be mutually taken in hand by Jews and Christians, so that a society may be formed whose object it would be to undertake the solving of the question. Should this united society of Jews and Christians be formed, then an important step has been already taken.

II. It would be well if the society adopt three principal rules —UNITY, FREEDOM, and LOVE—for its programme.

(a.) *Unity* with regard to the conflicts between nation and nation, or between Jews and Gentiles, and for our motto should be preached diligently to Jews and Christians: "Have we not all one Father? hath not one God created us? why do we deal treacherously every man against his brother?" (Mal. ii. 10).

(b.) *Freedom of thought* in regard to belief and religion, so that one may not condemn the other because one thinks differently from the other; for only through peace and liberty are we able to forward the welfare of mankind; and freedom alone can lead us in the right way. None should hate another for his belief; and the free interchange of thought in things pertaining to belief should not draw hatred after it.

(c.) *Love* in all social dealings. Every member should devote himself with self-denial to work for the common good.

True philosophy knows no other God than the God who is Love, and the Holy Scriptures teach us that he who has no love does not know God (1 John iv. 18). Love produces everything good in nature, and where love does not reign, there is destruction and desolation. Therefore, love must inspire the work which it imposes upon itself, namely, to unite all the children of one Father as brethren.

III. The society shall endeavour to form sub-committees in all possible places, which shall hold active communication with the general committee, to whom they shall report the social intercourse between Jews and Christians.

These sub-committees must carefully study the local circumstances, and lay clearly before the general committee all causes of dispute, and propose such methods as would settle them and foster union and peace among the inhabitants. Every sub-committee must have its own special methods; for we cannot put side by side the Jews and Christians of Britain, France, Germany, and other civilised countries, with those of Russia, Poland, and the East.

IV. The society shall have a journal in different languages, as their organ, which shall be the means of promoting concord among the nations, and of drawing them nearer to each other.

Although my methods were in general favourably received, they have been criticised in various ways. I did not mean to say that my proposals are the only right ones, but, as I said in my second pamphlet, if any one knows better methods, let him propound them, instead of criticising the plans of others.

Many Jews thought that the Jewish question should be called the Christian question, and that the Christians should be reminded of peace. I called that question by the name under which it is known. Supposing we agree that we have to impress upon the Christians that it lies alone and entirely upon their side, then may those Jews furnish the practicable method which could be applied to the Christians. A sterile polemic, abusing and blaming one another, is certainly not the right way to improve the condition of the Jews. One can indeed incite feeling with evil words, but that can in no way bring about a reconciliation. Paper quarrels will never bring about a reconciliation between Jews and Christians. The true Christian takes a lively interest in the prosperity of his Jewish fellow citizen, and strongly condemns the excesses of that fanatical rabble which, with deadly hatred, persecutes all those who do not belong to it.

In Germany many Christians have lifted up their voices in favour of the persecuted Jews, as there were found Christians with the true Christian religion of love in their hearts. A Christian question, therefore, this anti-Semitic agitation can not be called; for you will not find a true Christian engaged in it; but you will find orthodox Catholics, fanatic Lutherans, and above all, Atheists, in the latter of whom the Jews thought to find their best friends; now, however, they can see, that only those who love Christ in sincerity, and who study His Holy Word diligently, are their real friends.

Having expressed my views clearly upon the Jewish question, I shall now give the opinions of others, which I received in answer to my circular upon this subject. Dr. Fürst writes:—

"MY DEAR SIR,—In thanking you for your circular and the first number of the 'Judenfrage' kindly forwarded to me, I cannot help expressing to you my hearty sympathy in the noble and important work you have undertaken.

"The paper of Mr. Folticineano has interested me very much, as it not only contains many important suggestions and impartial statements, but is written in a conciliatory spirit, in harmony with the subject treated. It does one good to see an intelligent Jew breathing a spirit of love and goodwill; not only towards his own nation, but to all men without distinction. Thus his important paper, more than anything else, has convinced me that it is your duty and privilege to confine your truly philanthropic efforts exclusively to Roumania. He has pointed out what there is still to be done among these 400,000 Jews and five and a-half millions of Gentiles. If you endeavour to raise the Jews there, and try to bring about a reconciliation between them and their Christian countrymen, you have a task before you requiring all your time and energy, and all the help you can get. If you succeed in effecting such a great and beneficial result, it will more than compensate you for all the labour you may have bestowed upon it.

"Wishing you God's blessing on all your efforts for the good of others,—I remain, my dear Sir, yours very truly,

"Dr. A. FÜRST.

"STRASBOURG, 12th July, 1881."

The paper of Mr. Folticineano, to which Dr. Fürst

alludes, is an answer to my circular, and I would give it here, but it is rather too long, being not less than twenty-one printed pages. I have printed it in German in my first issue of the pamphlet "Die Judenfrage."

I am indebted to the eminent professor, Dr. Paulus Cassel of Berlin, for a very interesting letter on this subject, which I shall insert here :—

"MY DEAR MR. BASSIN,—With this letter I send you my pamphlet 'Die Antisemiten und die Christliche Kirche.' You will therein find the momentousness of the present Jewish agitation. I also draw your attention to my previous publications 'Sendshreiben an Heinrich von Freitshke' and 'Die Juden in der Weltgeschichte.' I have treated this subject for years in my periodical *Sunem*. What I think about the whole affair is no secret in Germany, nor, I think, in England. There was always a Jewish question, but only in so far as it was asked, How is it possible that there are yet any Jews, although they have lived in the midst of Christians for centuries? The answer was, that so many Jews remaining explained itself by so much *heathendom* remaining among the nations. And what is called the Jewish question, is in fact nothing more than heathenish hatred against the Jews. The question of the agitators is not one of spirit and belief, but of money. Instead of seeking to subdue a false prejudice, they rather inflame it. They have no other encouragement thereto than knowing that they are in the majority.

"What the Bohemians in Prague do to the Germans, and the French in Marseilles to the Italians, will others do to the Jews. In the latter case, they think of the villas and the incomes which they have in the large towns. It is a sign of still existing political roughness which makes itself notorious towards a minority. Means against it are found only in the proper and moral education through the Gospel. There is no other means than the sword of authority, which only checks violent acts for the moment. This gospel includes the humanity with which one suffers and endures. It acknowledges the right of others to live on God's earth, as well as those who are themselves Christians. It is her duty, through her presence, to elevate and improve others. She gives the sword to authority, to punish and prevent evil; but she takes the arbitrariness of the majority which offers violence to others, plunders them, and drives them out.

"The Jewish question is the Christian question; it is also a culture question.

"From the condition of the Jews one can draw a conclusion of the people among whom they live. They have been persecuted for 1500 years, and have endured it, and gained much thereby. It was time to let them experience humanity and justice. But after a short tranquillity in some countries, comes again the anti-Semitic animosity rougher than ever; a false religious zeal because without pathos. Such can bring no blessing, and least to the persecutors. Hatred is a seed which always brings corrupt fruit. It can never be justified; one can have no agreement or transaction with it; endeavours after conciliation with it are impossible. No assembly in the world can otherwise determine what would bring mankind together more than self-knowledge and love.

"The sickle that would cut off the growth of Christendom, they put to that of the Jews. The love which one claims for himself, he should also show to others. When Christ rejected the Pharisees, He meant not only those in Jerusalem alone; when He had compassion on the Samaritan woman, so surely, also, on the sick in Israel. Should He approach that roaring rabble, as they appear in Berlin and elsewhere, He would take them for His murderers coming to crucify Him anew. He has been rejected, but He has not rejected Israel. He speaks: 'Go forth and teach that I am Love.'"

I think the impartial answer of Mr. Butynski, a Russian orthodox Jew, of Kowno, will also be read with interest:—

"*To the Rev.* ELIESER BASSIN, *Missionary in Jassy, Roumania.*

"Honoured and invited by your circular, permit me to address to you my sincere opinion upon your recent movement of the 'Jewish Question.' Without having the honour of personal acquaintance with you, I hope you will make the best use of these lines, such as they are.

" In the first place, I acknowledge that I belong to the orthodox Jewish party. Independently of our belief in an expected Messiah, I am convinced that the Jewish race, after having happily escaped extermination by the Philistines, Babylonians, Greeks, and Romans, and endured inquisitions and crusades, can never be rooted out by brutal or non-intelligent persecution. Let the promoting of fraternal disunion and of the fury of the mob be ever so base and cruel, it can only partly injure Israel outwardly for a time; the inner germ of the priestly holy people ever reappears like a phœnix out of the ashes.

" I contend further, that, as you say in your circular, 'the Jew cannot cease to be hated by the nations until he become changed,' is to be understood not in the sense of your mission; otherwise we must reason upon other grounds. 'The Jew is *conservative;*' is he so in religious matters? And if so, whom does he harm with it? The most modern Jews are no less political and social than conservative, and this is again a cause for complaint against them.

" 'He is hated by the nations.' Is he not much more envied and feared on account of his abilities and endurance?

" How far the Jew may be a stumbling-block to all nations depends npon how the matter is regarded. Naturally *Lassalle* and *Carl Marx* are stumbling-blocks to great manufacturers, as also *Lasker* is to a high-standing *Wagner and Co.;* as, on the other hand, a usurer is to a spendthrift noble, and a publican to a drunken artisan. But how can individual accusations fall upon a whole nation?

" That a change must take place amongst the Jews is unfortunately very true! They have in the last centuries adopted fearful social vices, from which the sooner they are purged the better. Let the responsibility fall on those who forced that people to these vices, as a cast-out, persecuted step-child is forced to lying, stealing, and other crimes.

" Now, to your two questions, which, indeed, are but one. The only and most practical advice is that the clergy, preachers, journalists, officials, and all those who have any influence upon national and public opinion, and who mean conscientiously, faithfully, and honestly by mankind, should use all their eloquence to avert the nation from a terrible prejudice against the Jews, for the genuine mind finds its allies in the real instinct of the nation; and opposed to this, the enmity of the instigator is powerless, and the Jewish question will be solved.

"Virtues and vices are to be found amongst the Jews as well as among other nations; but no one may attribute the crime of one individual to a whole nation, and call forth a crusade against it!

"To your concluding verse from Malachi, we can subjoin a corresponding quotation from the Talmud: 'O Heaven! are we not your brothers, the children of one father, the children of one mother? Whereby are we separated from all nations and tongues that you determined so much evil upon us'—(*Taanith*, xviii. 1).—With greatest esteem,

"J. BUTYNSKI.

"KOVNO, 10*th* (22*nd*) *June*, 1881."

I must not omit to give the opinion of Professor Dr. Delitzsch on this question, as he is a great friend of the Jews:—

"LEIPSIC, 11*th July*, 1881.

"ESTEEMED FRIEND,—I am unable to satisfy all my correspondence. What I think of the Jewish question will be seen from the work I send you.* The most sympathising seems to me to be the work of Professor Gran in Konigsberg, 'Die Judenfrage, ein Geheimniss?' I am so over-burdened that I must ask your indulgence....

"The new Prussian journal, the *Kreuz*, in a well-meant notice, regrets that in my work I did not also endeavour to communicate my thoughts upon the solving of the Jewish question. I have already done so elsewhere.

"There is nothing to be done by way of administration. One cannot lawfully close the paths of competition to the Jews which been opened for them by the law. The talents, and in a measure also the virtues, by means of which they always push further onwards and upwards, cannot be destroyed. The broken-down

---

* Rohling's *Talmudjude*, beleuchtet von Franz Delitzsch. [The Author.]

barriers cannot be restored. The anti-Semitic petition is a powerless protest, which only increases the opposition.

"How so? We say to the Jew, 'Be humble; do not push yourself so forward; and, before everything else, cease to scorn Christianity, and to praise the religion of your nation as the highest, whereas it was only a preparatory step to Christianity.' And we say to the Christians, 'See the consequences of your backsliding. You have unchristianised the oath, matrimony, and the schools in favour of the Jews. Your uncircumcised rabbis have struck out the Messiah from the Old Testament, and the miracle from the history of salvation. Who among you understands the 53rd chapter of Isaiah, about the One in whom Israel's history attains its summit, and who offered Himself for His people and for all nations? The Talmud is more Christian than you are, for Talmud and Midrasch teach how Wünsche in his work, *Die Leiden des Messias* (1870), has shown a suffering Christ. And the Talmud affirms that Jesus did wonders through the power of the most holy name of God. Your exegetes, your biographers of Jesus, have forged weapons for the Jews. The Jewish literature over which you now cry murder is become strong and of full age in the bosom of your celebrated classics. You have lost your crown, but it is not the Jews who have robbed you of it. You have sacrificed it yourselves for the Thyrsus of the 'Religion in the Time of Darwin.' From this backsliding there is no other way of return but by repentance. If this call should find a mutual hearing, then would a tolerable *modus vivendi* be formed, and that is for the present the only possible solution of the Jewish question.

"But we, the representatives of the Jewish Mission, we who make love to Israel inaccessible to national hatred, will not cease to appease both sides. We point the Radicals to the God of universal history. We know His ways from the word of prophecy; He makes even the wicked useful to Himself, but woe to those who unchain the evil one.—Your brother in Christ,

"DELITZSCH."

CHAPTER XXI.

THE JOURNAL "EINTRACHT;" INTERVIEW ON THE WAY TO GREAT BRITAIN WITH REV. D. EDWARD, PROFESSOR DR. PAULUS CASSEL, AND OTHER FRIENDS, CONCERNING THE JOURNALS "EINTRACHT" AND "CONCORDIA;" ARRIVAL IN LONDON; CONSULTATION WITH MY FRIENDS DR. BENOLY AND DR. KOPPEL; ARRIVAL IN EDINBURGH; RESOLUTION OF THE JEWISH MISSION COMMITTEE; MY RETURN TO JASSY POSTPONED.

WHO has never felt in his breast a disinterested desire to render useful service to mankind? Who has never in his leisure hours reflected upon the proceedings of the world? and in whose imagination has not existed an ideal of human peace and happiness? In such moments I determined to publish a weekly journal in German, under the title of *Eintracht*, and to urge in it the settling of the quarrel between Jews and Christians, and, with the assistance of all noble thinkers, to endeavour to find the right way to do so.

On 9th September, 1881, I issued the first number. The journal was favourably received by most Jews and Christians over the whole world, and was also recommended by many Jewish and Christian papers. The *Jewish Chronicle* in London was the only one that I am aware of, that was not in favour of it, and in its issue of 30th September, 1881, appeared the following:—

"*Roumania.*—A notorious missionary in Jassy, named Bassin, has brought out a journal under the title of *Eintracht,* which, whilst professing to defend Jewish interests, is really intended to catch Jewish souls. Bassin announces that after the 1st October the journal will be published in London. How necessary it is to warn the Roumanian Jews against this paper, whose real object is artfully concealed, is shown by the fact that even the editor of the *Archives Israelites* of Paris has fallen into the trap, and favourably commends the paper as an excellent Jewish organ."

However, this did not discourage me, for I knew that the editor of the *Jewish Chronicle* is not better than the most Jews, who, having no confidence in the Christians, believe that everything that comes through a missionary must have some hidden motive; they cannot understand that he is moved only by pure love for his fellow-creatures, and that he sympathises with them in their persecutions.

Uncertain as to whether the Free Church of Scotland would take up Roumania as a mission field, and believing that the Lord called me to work for the welfare of humanity in general and of the Jews in particular, I resolved to return to Great Britain, and to edit in London the *Eintracht* in German and the *Concordia* in English. It was also in my mind to establish a society, of which I made mention in the foregoing chapter.

Accordingly, I left Jassy early in October, 1881. In Breslau, I visited Rev. D. Edward, who advised me to go first to Edinburgh, to have an interview with the Jewish Mission Committee, and, if they should decide upon taking up Roumania as a Jewish mission field, then to return to Jassy and engage in the work to which the Lord called me. My friend, Professor

Paulus Cassel, whom I visited in Berlin, was also of the same opinion. In London I took counsel with my friends, Dr. Benoly and Dr. Koppel, and we agreed that I should go first to Edinburgh. The Rev. R. Koenig of Pesth, whom I met in London, also advised me to see the Committee. I therefore set out for Scotland, and arrived in Edinburgh, 12th October, 1881.

At the Committee meeting on the 18th, a resolution was passed that I should return at once to Jassy. The conditions were not very encouraging to me, but after earnest prayer, I resolved to accept everything that came from the Committee as from the hand of God, and I besought the Lord that He would guide them to do what should be the best for His kingdom. I therefore sent a letter to the Committee, requesting permission to remain for the winter in Scotland, in order to have Christian intercourse, and to attend the theological classes in the New College, which would be a step towards my ordination. In compliance with this request, the Committee, at their meeting in November, decided that my return to Jassy should be postponed till the end of March, 1882. The Jewish Mission Committees of March and April, resolved to postpone my return to Roumania till after the General Assembly of 1882, and to recommend cordially to the Presbytery of Edinburgh, my application for license. The Free Presbytery of Edinburgh unanimously agreed to transmit said application to the most favourable consideration of the General Assembly. On the report of the Committee of the General Assembly, my petition was granted, and the said

Assembly enjoined the Presbytery of Edinburgh to license me, which they did on the 14th of June, 1882.

Although I am very glad that, by being licensed, I am called or empowered by the Church to preach the Gospel, yet my greatest happiness is that I am able to say with the Apostle (Gal. i. 1), that I was first called to preach the Gospel "not of men, neither by man, but by Jesus Christ and God the Father."

I have enjoyed many evidences of the warm sympathy of the Free Church of Scotland, especially during the time I attended the New College in Edinburgh. With the professors, with my fellow-students, and with friends in all parts of the country, I have enjoyed pleasant and profitable Christian fellowship, the memory of which will often cheer and sustain me in the mission field to which the Free Church, under God, now sends me.

What I said in my address to the General Assembly of 1882, I would now repeat, that I go to my mission work in Roumania with the motto—"Ora et labora," "Pray and Work," and I ask all the children of God to pray for me and my work.

THE END.

LORIMER AND GILLIES, PRINTERS, 31 ST. ANDREW SQUARE, EDINBURGH.

Lightning Source UK Ltd.
Milton Keynes UK
UKHW010929020119
334667UK00006B/552/P